School Rumble

Jin Kobayashi

TRANSLATED AND ADAPTED BY
William Flanagan

LETTERED BY
Dana Hayward

BALLANTINE BOOKS • NEW YORK

A Del Rey Trade Paperback Original

School Rumble 1 Copyright © 2003 by Jin Kobayashi
English translation copyright © 2006 by Jin Kobayashi

Publishing Group, a division of Random House, Inc., New York.
Published in the United States by Del Rey Books, an imprint of The Random House

Del Rey is a registered trademark and the Del Rey colophon is a trademark of Random House, Inc.

Publication rights arranged through Kodansha Ltd.

First published in Japan in 2003 by Kodansha Ltd., Tokyo

Library of Congress Control Number: 2006900277

ISBN 0-345-49147-5

Printed in the United States of America

www.delreymanga.com

9 8 7 6 5 4 3 2 1

Lettering—Dana Hayward

Honorifics

Throughout the Del Rey Manga books, you will find Japanese honorifics left intact in the translations. For those not familiar with how the Japanese use honorifics, and more important, how they differ from American honorifics, we present this brief overview.

Politeness has always been a critical facet of Japanese culture. Ever since the feudal era, when Japan was a highly stratified society, use of honorifics—which can be defined as polite speech that indicates relationship or status—has played an essential role in the Japanese language. When addressing someone in Japanese, an honorific usually takes the form of a suffix attached to one's name (example: "Asuna-san"), or as a title at the end of one's name or in place of the name itself (example: "Negi-sensei," or simply "Sensei!").

Honorifics can be expressions of respect or endearment. In the context of manga and anime, honorifics give insight into the nature of the relationship between characters. Many translations into English leave out these important honorifics, and therefore distort the "feel" of the original Japanese. Because Japanese honorifics contain nuances that English honorifics lack, it is our policy at Del Rey not to translate them. Here, instead, is a guide to some of the honorifics you may encounter in Del Rey Manga.

-*san*: This is the most common honorific, and is equivalent to Mr., Miss, Ms., Mrs., etc. It is the all-purpose honorific and can be used in any situation where politeness is required.

-*sama*: This is one level higher than "-san" and it is used to confer great respect.

-*dono*: This comes from the word "tono," which means "lord." It is an even higher level than "-sama," and confers utmost respect.

-*kun*: This suffix is used at the end of boys' names to express familiarity or endearment. It is also sometimes used by men among friends, or when addressing someone younger or of a lower station.

-chan: This is used to express endearment, mostly toward girls. It is also used for little boys, pets, and even among lovers. It gives a sense of childish cuteness.

Bozu: This is an informal way to refer to a boy, similar to the English term "kid" or "squirt."

Sempai/senpai: This title suggests that the addressee is one's "senior" in a group or organization. It is most often used in a school setting, where underclassmen refer to their upperclassmen as "sempai." It can also be used in the workplace, such as when a newer employee addresses an employee who has seniority in the company.

Kohai: This is the opposite of "sempai," and is used toward underclassmen in school or newcomers in the workplace. It connotes that the addressee is of lower station.

Sensei: Literally meaning "one who has come before," this title is used for teachers, doctors, or masters of any profession or art.

Nee-chan/Nii-chan: Older siblings are not commonly called by name but rather by the title "older sister" (*nee-chan*) or "older brother" (*nii-chan*). These honorifics can also be used with someone unrelated, when the relationship seems like a sibling relationship.

[blank]: Usually forgotten in these lists, but perhaps the most significant difference between Japanese and English. The lack of honorific means that the speaker has permission to address the person in a very intimate way. Usually, only family, spouses, or very close friends have this kind of permission. Known as *yobisute,* it can be gratifying when someone who has earned the intimacy starts to call one by one's name without an honorific. But when that intimacy hasn't been earned, it can be very insulting.

Cultural Note

To preserve some of the humor found in *School Rumble*, we have elected to keep Japanese names in their original Japanese order—that is to say, with the family name first, followed by the personal name. So when you hear the name Tsukamoto Tenma, Tenma is just one member of the Tsukamoto family.

WHAT THE HECK IS *LOVE?*

SMILE FOR ME!

A DREAM...?

I WANT TO BE WITH YOU ALWAYS.

I KNOW.

IT MAKES ME SO MAD!

BECAUSE I'M STRESSED OVER IT.

I'M SO HAPPY!

I'LL SAY IT, AND THEN YOU'LL SEE!

IT'S LIKE YOU'RE NOT AFRAID OF ANYTHING!

IT JUST GIVES ME THE CHILLS!

I WANT TO RUN AWAY SO BAD!

THAT'S WHAT THEY CALL FOOLING YOURSELF!

IT WAS USELESS FROM THE START.

I JUST DON'T UNDERSTAND BOYS!

THAT'S THE FIRST TIME I'VE HEARD THAT!

THIS REALLY HURTS!

DO YOU THINK I'M PRETTY?

I BELIEVE IN YOU, YOU KNOW!

AH HA HA HA!

IDIOT!

I CAN'T SLEEP.

WAS THAT AGAINST THE RULES?

OHH, NOO! WHAT'LL I DO?!

IT JUST COMES INTO MY BRAIN.

JUST ACCEPT IT!

AND YOU CALL YOURSELF A LADY?!

THIS JUST ISN'T LIKE ME!

School Rumble

1

Jin Kobayashi

IT ISN'T AN EXCUSE!

IS THAT A STAB IN THE BACK?

JUST TAKE A LOOK AT YOURSELF!

I LOVE YOU!!

I'M THE ONE WHO SHOULD BE CRYING!

I'M GIVING THIS MY BEST!

Are there feelings that you can't feel?

School Rumble

Contents

ONE DAY
I'LL SAY
IT...

THAT
YOU'RE
THE
REASON
I'M SO
HAPPY!

WHAT A WEIRD WORD!

LOVE...

#01 PLAN1 FROM OUTERSPACE

THE NEW SCHOOL YEAR BEGINS TODAY!

AND I'M GONNA GIVE IT MY BEST!!

SHKK

I'M A SECOND-YEAR STUDENT NOW...

ぴこん.. POING

RIGHT!

One could call her a normal high school student.

SORRY TO MAKE YOU WAIT!

Younger Sister Yakumo.

YOU'RE LATE!

Her name is Tsukamoto Tenma.

And like so many other girls around her age...

...she's fallen for a guy.

...ŌJI-KUN!!

It looks like she said it out loud.

IT'S KARA-SUMA...

BEEP-BEEP

AH!

Today is the day that class assignments come out, so for Tenma, this is the pivotal day on which her destiny turns.

I HOPE WE END UP IN THE SAME CLASS!

CLASS ASSIGNMENTS

OHHH!

ALL RIGHT!

OKAY!

WHAT ABOUT KARASUMA-SAN?

I HAVEN'T SEEN HIM YET.

NEE-CHAN, YOU'RE IN CLASS 2-C.

B-BMP

IF YOU'RE TOO SCARED, I CAN GO LOOK.

......

FIDGET FIDGET

WHOOSH

DON'T TALK NON-SENSE!!

烏丸大路

Karasuma Ôji

CON-GRATS.

SHAKK

WE'RE IN THE SAME CLASS !!!

ALL RIGHT!!

HEY! WE'RE IN THE SAME CLASS!

LET'S MAKE THIS A GREAT YEAR, KARASUMA-KUN!!

?

THAT'D BE FINE, BUT...

ペコ BOW BOW

...I'M TRANSFER-RING TO ANOTHER SCHOOL THE DAY AFTER TO-MORROW.

I'LL MAKE IT WORK OUT!!

THAT DREAM DIDN'T LAST LONG.

YOU'RE STILL AT IT?

Tenma's House

FIRST I'LL START CLEANING. THAT'LL CALM ME DOWN.

VWOOOM

うぃーん

THEN I'LL WASH DISHES!

5 hours later.

3 hours later.

THEN I'LL DO LAUNDRY AND CONSIDER MY OPTIONS!

KLONK コトッ KLONK

I'LL JUST SLEEP.

OH, HECK!

I CAN'T THINK OF ANYTHING!!

8 hours later.

AND...

...IS THAT ALL I'M PLANNING ON DOING?!

FFT

OR ELSE...

IF I'M GOING TO START HAVING REGRETS, THEN NOT DOING ANYTHING NOW IS THE PERFECT REGRET TO BEGIN WITH!

I NEVER DID ANYTHING TO LET HIM KNOW!

KARASUMA-KUN HAS NO IDEA HOW I FEEL!

SURE, I'M AFRAID! IT'S ONLY NATURAL!

I'LL LET HIM KNOW HOW I FEEL!

FIP

ALL I HAVE TO DO IS WRITE, "I LOVE YOU."

THAT SHOULD BE EASY! EASY! ♥

BUT I HAVE NO IDEA HOW A PERSON DOES THAT!

FIRST THING IS TO WRITE HIM A LOVE LETTER, RIGHT?

...LOAD MY STUFF TO GO INTO THE MOUNTAINS TO WATCH YOU SKI!

WHAT THE HECK AM I WRITING?!

POFF

ZOOM ZOOM

DEAR KARASUMA-KUN, I LO... ...LO...

...LO...

...

...LO...

— 11 —

I LOST MY PEN

... LO ...

D-DEAR KARASUMA-KUN, I...

NOTHING! NOTHING IS UP!!

HEY, NEE-CHAN? WHAT'S UP?

...LOATHE SUKIYAKI!!

DEAR KARASUMA-KUN, I...

CALM DOWN, TENMA! CALM DOWN!

NEE-CHAN, ARE YOU TALKING IN YOUR SLEEP?!

WHY CAN'T I GET TO THE POINT?!

LONGITUDE!

LOYALTY!

In a voice getting more and more stressed.

I LODGE MYSELF IN YOUR DOORWAY!

I LOWER MY DEFENSES!

The next day...

WHAT'LL I DO? WHAT'LL I DO?

I CAN'T WRITE IT!

WHAMM

TREMBLE

SOMEHOW IT JUST FEELS WRONG!

WHO'D EVER READ ALL THIS?!

I DON'T CARE WHAT THE WORDS ARE, I JUST HAVE TO LET HIM KNOW HOW I FEEL!

OH, FOR–

To Karasuma-kun.

...IT CAME OUT IN THE FORM OF A SCROLL.

AND IN THE END...

KARASUMA

パタン...
KACHIK

I DID THE BEST I COULD ON IT.

THIS IS OKAY.

HA HA!

HA HH HH...

SEE YA.

CHATTER

SORRY, I HAVE MY CLUB RIGHT NOW.

CHATTER

HE'S READING IT!!

HE...
.....

SHLOOM

SHLOOM

SHLOOM

HE'S STILL READING IT!

SHUUUSSH

As the sun sinks into the west...

HE...
.....

SHLOOM

OKAY. NOW...

HE'S READING IT AGAIN!!

POING

SHLOOM SHLOOM

I'M SORRY IT WAS SO LONG!

AH! IT LOOKS LIKE HE'S FINISHED...

HE'S ROLLING IT UP AGAIN.

And as evening turns to night...

AWOOO!

HMM...

.....

SHLOOM SHLOOM

I-IT LOOKS LIKE HE'S FINISHED.

HE'S ROLLING IT UP AGAIN.

HAHHHH...

DO YOU THINK HE LIKED WHAT HE SAW?!

IS THAT KARASUMA-KUN'S REACTION?!

OH, NOOO!!!

I *THOUGHT* THE PERSON NEVER MENTIONED HER NAME.

IT'S OVER...

MY FIRST LOVE...!!

WHA...?!

HOW?!
HOW DID IT
HAPPEN?!

じゃりっ
BAM

DO YOU
KNOW THAT
GUY,
KARASUMA-
KUN?

THEY
SAY HE
DELAYED
HIS
TRANSFER.

*But
soon...*

HE GOT
PERMISSION
FROM HIS
PARENTS TO
STAY HERE
ANOTHER
YEAR.

...I HEARD
THAT SOMEONE
ASKED HIM TO
STAY.

*Don't go
away!
Please,
don't go!*

I DON'T
KNOW MUCH
ABOUT IT,
BUT...

I DON'T
KNOW.

01 .... Fin.

02 EASY RIDER

I'M JUST WHAT I LOOK LIKE, A JUVENILE DELINQUENT HIGH SCHOOL STUDENT.

At school...

MY NAME'S HARIMA KENJI.

I CAN'T BELIEVE IT'S MORNING ALREADY!

GLANCE

IT'S TSUKAMOTO TENMA-CHAN!!

Yet another one who is in love.

HARIMA! HOW DARE YOU COME TO SCHOOL DRESSED LIKE THAT—

SKROW

THONK

I WANT HER TO BE IN *MY* CLASS!

A newly hired teacher.

HEAVEN TO HELL

Harima Kenji: *A Man Who Loves From Afar.*

CLASS ASSIGNMENTS

CLASS ASSIGNMENTS

FOR TEN SECONDS, I'LL PUT ALL MY THOUGHTS INTO IT...

...INTO PLACING ME INTO CLASS 2-C!

GRIMP

MY THOUGHTS!

DON'T MEET HIS EYES, YOU IDIOT!

HEY, IT'S HARIMA! IT'S THE FIRST TIME I'VE EVER SEEN HIM!

......

MURMUR

Takano Akira

Tsukamoto Tenma

...IN CLASS 2-C!!

Tonami Yoshiko

TENMA-CHAN IS...

---

1 !!

4
3
2
...

PLACE ME IN 2-C! PLACE ME IN 2-C! PLACE ME IN 2-C! PLACE ME IN 2-C!

PLACE ME IN 2-C! PLACE ME IN 2-C! PLACE ME IN 2-C! PLACE ME IN 2-C!

CHATTER CHATTER

MUMBLE

MUMBLE

CHATTER CHATTER

8
7

10
9

I SAW YER NAME!

YER IN CLASS 2-D, AREN'TCHA, KENJI-SAN?!

YOU ACTUALLY CAME TO SCHOOL, HUH?

YO, KENJI-SAN!

HOW'S IT GOIN'?

CLASS 2-D, YOU SAY? HARIMA KENJI IS IN...

Hamada Tosh...
Harry McKenzie
Hokunara Ruiko

WH-**WHAT** WAS THAT, KENJI-SAN...?

THAT'S WHAT HAPPENS WHEN MY THOUGHT POWER HAS NOWHERE TO GO.

YOU SEE HOW MUCH POWER MY THOUGHTS HAVE?

I'M SORRY! I JUMPED TO CONCLUSIONS!

GIMME BACK MY THOUGHT POWER!

I WANT IT BACK...

YOU PUNK! YOUR JOKES ARE *TOO* GOOD!

THAT'S SOME FOR-EIGNER!!

YOU'RE ONE STUPID PUNK! YOU SHOULD LEARN FROM ME!

GEEZ!

CLASS ASSIGNMENTS

I'M GONNA LOOK AT THE WHOLE CHART AND FIND MY NAME IN ONE GO!

HM... 2-C, HUH?

SHKK

After looking many, many times...

RUBB RUBB

MMM...

WHAT'S THIS?

GONNNG

MY NAME ISN'T THERE AT ALL!!

Looks at Class F.

Looks at Class R.

DAMMIT! JUST WHAT CLASS AM I SUPPOSED TO BE IN?!

NOW I REMEMBER!!

WHAT ARE *YOU* DOING HERE?

YOU WERE SUSPENDED FOR THIS YEAR!!

#02.........Fin.

HARIMA!

HUH...? IT ISN'T THERE!

WHERE'S MY NAME?

Tsukamoto Tenma found herself in the same class as Karasuma Ōji.

The classes' assignments have been decided.

...that doesn't mean that Tenma's battle is over.

How-ever...

ANY-WAY...

TONK TONK

Homeroom teacher.

WE'LL TAKE CARE OF SEAT ASSIGNMENTS TOMORROW, OKAY?

POING

Homeroom period.

I MUST FIND A WAY TO SIT NEAR KARASUMA-KUN!

GAMPH

YOU'D BE BETTER OFF TAKING YOUR BATH AND GOING TO BED.

CAN'T YOU SEE YOUR OLDER SISTER IS IN LOVE?!

KA-CHNK

IN THE FIRST PLACE, I DON'T SEE WHAT THE FUSS IS ABOUT!

SEAT ASSIGNMENTS ARE NOTHING MORE THAN LUCK.

SHHHHH

That evening ...

...A HIGH SCHOOL STUDENT.

BUT REALLY, I'M ...

SLP

I'M TREATED LIKE A KID!

SO I HAVE TO DO AS MUCH AS I CAN ABOUT THIS!

MMM...
.....
.....
...MM!

SO...

ZU!!
BI!!
SWAMM

A STAR!!
THE MARKING ON THAT CARD IS A STAR!!

BWIMM

UMF!

AND I HAVE NO PROBLEMS BENDING SPOONS!

EVEN THOUGH I READ EVERY WORD IN THE BOOK!

OH, HONESTLY! WHAT IS THIS?!

I CAN'T EVEN GET IT RIGHT ONCE!

E.S.P.

KARASUMA-KUN!

SIGH

DEPRESSION IS NOT AN OPTION!

I JUST DON'T HAVE TIME FOR IT!

WHOOSH

NOT AT ALL!! *EMOTIONS* ARE AT THE HEART OF THE MATTER! I HAVE A FEELING MY LUCK IS ABOUT TO GET A BIG BOOST!

SO YOU *ARE* SERIOUS, HUH?

LOOKING AT YOU, I GET A FEELING FOR HOW FUTILE EVERYTHING IS.

IN THE END, NOTHING WORKED.

The next day...

WHAAAAA...

WAIT! I CHANGED MY MIND! I *DON'T* WANT TO HEAR IT.

IT... IT WAS... IT WAS THE HORO-SCOPE THEY SHOWED THIS MORNING ON TV.

TODAY OF ALL DAYS!

• • • •

WHAT'S CAUSING TODAY'S GREAT LUCK?

OKAY...

UM... KARASUMA-KUN IS WHERE, EXACTLY?

WITH THAT MANY SEATS TO CHOOSE FROM...

2 - C

RIGHT... FOR THE SEAT ASSIGNMENTS...

MY FIRST CHOICE IS BEHIND, THEN SIDE-BY-SIDE, THEN KITTY-CORNER BEHIND, THEN IN FRONT, THEN KITTY-CORNER IN FRONT!

A WINDOW SEAT IN THE LAST ROW?!

MY OPTIONS ARE SUDDENLY SO LIMITED!!

THE ONLY ONE LEFT IS THE SEAT IN FRONT OF HIM!

THE NUMBER I HAVE TO DRAW IS 6!!

TSUKA-MOTO-SAN, YOU'RE NEXT.

PICK A NUMBER.

B-BMP

B-BMP

B-BMP

FLIP

PLEASE! LET ME PICK 6!!

...FATE ITSELF!!

I JUST SAW A 6! BUT ISN'T THAT CHEATING? NO!! IT ISN'T A CHEAT, IT'S...

EH?

IT'S ALL MINE!!

HAYAAH!

WHUMPH

I'M RIGHT IN FRONT OF KARASUMA-KUN!

YAY! YAAYY! ♪

IT SURE IS.

THIS IS THE SEAT FOR 6, RIGHT?

BUT I JUST PULLED SEAT 6!

?

WAIT JUST A MINUTE HERE!!

YOU SEE THE LITTLE DOT?

THIS! RIGHT HERE.

HEY! DID YOU EVEN LOOK AT THIS?

EH?

!!

LET ME SEE THAT.

THAT TELLS YOU THAT YOU DREW A 9!!

DESCENT INTO THE VOIIIID

OH, NO, THEN WHERE IS 9?!

FRONT AND CENTER!

WELCOME TO THE TEACHER'S *SPECIAL* SEAT!

REALLY? I SUPPOSE... IS THERE ANYONE WHO'D BE WILLING TO CHANGE—

MY EYESIGHT HAS BEEN GETTING WORSE. COULD I HAVE A SEAT UP FRONT?

WHAT IS IT?

EXCUSE ME!

V-VERY WELL. TH-THEN IT'S DECIDED.

GRNNNNN

ME! I'LL DO IT! I'LL CHANGE WITH HIM! ME!!

I FEEL IT!

I CAN FEEL HIS WARM EYES WATCHING ME!

HEH HEH!

→ Looking out the window.

IT'S OKAY. I DID IT FOR MY OWN REASONS.

REALLY! THANK YOU SO MUCH!

03 . . . . Fin.

BONUS!

He was suspended for this year, but they made a special exception and allowed him to advance.

Harima Kenji.

Not only that, but they put him in Class 2-C also.

I AIN'T SEEIN' TOO GOOD, AND I'LL NEVER LEARN ANYTHING IF I SIT IN BACK.

ZWIP

HEY, I GOT A GOOD IDEA!

YOU MIND IF I TAKE YOUR FRONT-ROW SEAT?

EH...?

FINE WITH ME.

HM? THEY SEATED TENMA-CHAN IN THE FIRST ROW?

Seat Assignments...

MY SUNGLASSES! *THAT'S* WHY I COULDN'T SEE!

AH!

YOU SAY YOU'VE GOT BAD EYESIGHT, HARIMA?

HA HA HA

The guy who just switched with Tenma.

...

Kenji promised himself he wouldn't cause any trouble...

ALL RIGHT !!

......

Kenji's assigned seat is right next to Tenma.

#03 BONUS .... Fin.

NEE-CHAN,
YOU REALLY
SHOULDN'T ...

STATS:

Height: 166 cm (5' 5")

Favorite Thing: Sister

Least Favorite Thing: Dogs

Favorite Place: A bright, sunny veranda

Special Talent: Cooking, taking care of her sister

Hardest Thing to Live With: Will fall asleep anytime, anywhere

Notes: Can read the minds of people who have feelings for her

By the way, her cat's name is Iori.

Love
Letter.

STARRRE

Realizing how precarious her situation is, Tenma composes a love letter addressed to her intended boyfriend. Unfortunately, despite the extensive message, her plan resulted in failure. (She neglected to identify herself as the sender.)

Class 2-C. Karasuma Ôji is the object of Tsukamoto Tenma's affections. However, it is revealed that he is committed to transfer to a scholastic institute in America.

The answer would be that Karasuma requested a postponement of the transfer.

And yet, one may ask the reason why the dire situation took a turn for the better.

The Library . . .

I'M GOING TO BORROW IT RIGHT NOW!

FLIP

はら
はら！

FLIP

. . .IS *SUCH* A GREAT NAME FOR A NOVEL!

どろ

ぞろ

SNEAK AWAY

SNEAK AWAY

TSUKAMOTO TENMA'S BATTLE BEGINS THIS VERY MOMENT!!

ほー

THREE MINUTES LATER...

WHERE'D HE GO TO GET THAT STRAW HAT?

I HAVE TO LEARN EVERYTHING THERE IS TO KNOW!

I'LL TURN MY FAILURE INTO A SUCCESS!

WHUMP

PSYCHOLOGY OF HUMAN LOVE

I'M JUST BAD AT READING SMALL PRINT! OKAY, WHAT'S NEXT?

I'M SO DUMB!!

IS THIS THE LIMIT OF HOW MUCH KARASUMA-KUN MEANS TO YOU?!

PAFF PAFF

SCHNOOR SCHNOOR

POING POING

MMBL... KARASUMA-KUN... MMBL...

PAKK

GUWAAA!!

"IF YOU KNOW THE ENEMY AND KNOW YOURSELF, YOU NEED NOT FEAR THE RESULT OF A HUNDRED BATTLES."

THIS IS IT!!

THE ART OF WAR

SUN TSU

ASIDE FROM ROMANCE NOVELS, WHAT ELSE CAN I... OH!

"KNOW YOURSELF," HUH?

THAT MAKES SENSE! ONLY A WOMAN WOULD KNOW THE SOUL OF ANOTHER GIRL!

SON KO?
孫子？
そんこ
..... SO WHO WROTE THIS TREATISE?

JUST WHAT KIND OF GIRL AM I?

Tsukamoto Tenma: *Obsessive.*

ATHLETICS:

OW!

SUBSTANDARD.

SCHOLASTICS:

WHAT? WHAT? I GOTTA WRITE SOMETHING!

SUBSTANDARD.

THERE'S NOT A SINGLE GOOD THING ABOUT ME!

Looks and Style: Normal

Maybe...

Not the type to stand out in class.

Tsukamoto Tenma

Height: 154 cm (5' 1")
Weight: 43 kg (95 lbs)

FWAFF FWAFF

SHFF SHFF

もこ もこ

NOW, TO BUSINESS!

ZZZZIP

SHIFF

ntil the en
gives you a
opening, th
take off like
a hare, and it
ll be too la

TAKE OFF LIKE A HARE? TAKE OFF WHAT LIKE A HARE?

FLIP FLIP

THE ART OF W...

THE ART

LET'S SEE WHAT ELSE IT SAYS...

NO GIVING UP!

Tsukamoto Tenma: *Shy.*

IT MEANS TO RUN AWAY LIKE A RABBIT.

"TAKE OFF LIKE A HARE"?

OH! OF *COURSE* IT DOES!

WEIRD THOUGHTS ARE COMING FROM INSIDE ME!

SOMETHING IS DEFINITELY WRONG WITH THIS PICTURE!

COULD YOU TELL ME THE MEANING OF THIS PHRASE?

EXCUSE ME!

GNNGNNGNNGNN

HE'S RIGHT HERE!!

THANK YOU FOR YOUR HELP!

NOT AT ALL...

HE MUST HAVE COME WHILE I WAS SLEEPING!

HE MUST THINK I'M THE WEIRDEST PERSON IN THE WORLD!!

WHEN DID HE APPEAR THERE ?!

ZOOM

AH!

YES, EXACTLY LIKE THAT.

JUST LIKE A RABBIT.

Tsukamoto Tenma: *Something of a dolt.*

BUT... THAT WAS THE FIRST TIME KARASUMA-KUN TALKED TO ME, HUH?

KARASUMA-KUN... C-C-CAN YOU TELL ME HOW YOU SAY THIS WORD?!

GLINT

HERE! HERE!

The woman is getting carried away.

as your own **beloved** sons, and

SINCE THAT'S THE CASE, THEN I'LL ASK HIM TO PRONOUNCE THIS WORD!

DAMMIT! DAMMIT!! *DAMMIT!!!*

SAY, ARE YOU IN HIGH SCHOOL? ♡ YOU'RE PRETTY CUTE!

OH, THAT?

IT'S PRONOUNCED *BELOVED!*

HA HA HA BWA

TELL ME WHAT YOU GET WHEN YOU USE THIS!?

KARA-SUMA-KUN!

WHOOSH

MAYBE I CAN ASK HIM WHAT A BEE-KEEPER'S EXTRACTOR IS FOR AND GET HIM TO SAY "HONEY"!

FLIP-FLIP FLIP FLIP FLIP FLIP FLIP FLIP

Doesn't know when to give up.

THAT'S IT! HE'S GOING TO CALL ME...!!

UM...

I-GOT-THE-WRONG-PAGE!

FARM EQUIPMENT (Extended Edition)

Senba Koki (1000 Tooth Thresher)
An unusual development in ...period farm equipment, was used to

CHAFF.

YEAH! SEE YOU, KARASUMA-KUN!

POING

A woman who is quick to recover.

SO, I'LL SEE YOU LATER...

...TSUKA-MOTO-SAN.

POING

EXCUSE ME, BUT IT'S TIME FOR ME TO GO.

04 .... Fin.

#05 ENTER THE DRAGON

IT DOESN'T MATTER WHAT KIND OF TRASH HE MAY BE, WHEN A MAN IS IN LOVE...

...HE CAN'T LET ANYTHING BRING HIM LOW!

TH' SON OF A—

HERE HE COMES!

THIS IS WHAT LOVE IS!

HE REFUSES TO LOSE!

Don't think, FEEL——

WRONGO

EHH?

OKAY, PEOPLE! TO FIND OUT EVERY-ONE'S STRONG POINTS...

...I HAVE A SIMPLE TEST FOR YOU ALL TO TAKE.

Harima Kenji: Juvenile Delinquent.

BUT I GOT NO CHOICE! IT'S WHAT I GOTTA DO TO BE WITH TENMA-CHAN.

WHAT IS THIS? IS IT EVEN JAPANESE?

TSK! ON THE LIST OF THINGS I CAN DO WITHOUT, STUDY COMES RIGHT AFTER PEOPLE BLACK-MAILING ME!

HAVE YOU FORGOTTEN TO WRITE YOUR NAME?!

T-TENMA-CHAN! YOUR NAME!!

URK!!

!!

YEAR
CLASS
年　組
NAME
氏名

I CAN'T EVEN SPEAK TO WARN HER OF HER DANGER!

MAYBE SHE SIMPLY HASN'T NOTICED.

BUT WE'RE IN THE MIDDLE OF A TEST!

I'LL MOUTH THE WORDS TO HER!!

I ONLY HAVE ONE OPTION!

YOU · FOR · GOT · TO · WRITE · YOUR · NAME!

TEN · MA · CHAN!

FLAP FLAP

Harima Kenji: *Always in Sunglasses.*

TEN · MA · CHAN! YOUR · NAME! YOUR · NAME!!

I'LL YELL IT!!

FLAPPA FLAPPA

· · · · · ·

ALL RIGHT, THEN...

NO GOOD. MAYBE THE WORDS ARE TOO COMPLICATED FOR MOUTHING.

Harima Kenji: *Never Lost a Fight.*

TH, THERE MUST BE ANOTHER WAY! THERE MUST!!

WHAT AM I DOING? I'M JUST LOOKING LIKE A BIG GOLDFISH!

I'M SUCH AN IDIOT!!

HA HA HA! YOU'D BETTER TAKE MORE CARE, HARIMA.

MURMUR MURMUR

TSK! I MADE A FOOL OF MYSELF! BUT, IF IT ...

EVEN IF I HAD ANSWERED ALL THE QUESTIONS RIGHT, WHO WOULD HAVE KNOWN IT WAS ME? THAT WAS ONE CLOSE CALL!

OH, MY GOSH! I ALMOST FORGOT TO PUT MY NAME ON THE TEST.

I HAVE NO CHOICE! I HAVE TO USE THE STANDARD LIE!

I WAS TALKING ABOUT YOU!!

FIGURE IT OUT!

HAVEN'T YOU EVER HEARD OF LEARNING FROM OTHERS' MISTAKES?!

BUT SHE'S SO CUTE!!

TEE HEE

HEY, WAIT, JUST A SECOND!!

THAT SHOULD DO IT!

GULP

!?

OH! I'VE ALREADY DONE THAT LAST ENGLISH TRANSLATION QUESTION!

WHAT'S GOING ON? IT WAS WAY TOO EASY!

Getting desperate.

MAYBE I SHOULD PULL OUT ALL THE STOPS AND MAKE HER REALIZE!

SLIPP

答え (ANSWER)

You forgot to put down your name!

DID THAT DO THE TRICK?!

POFF

?

?

Harima Kenji: *Not a Lot of Friends.*

Harima Kenji: *Fool.*

IT COULD WORK!!

TSUKA MOTO TEN

I'VE DECIDED TO ACCEPT THIS MISSION!

YOU'LL SEE, TENMA-CHAN!

#05........FIN.

DINNER'S ALL READY!!

Yakumo introduces...

TSUKA MOTO TEN MA
塚本天満

STATS:

Height: 154 cm (5' 5")

Favorite Thing: Karasuma-san

Least Favorite Thing: She can't eat anything too spicy.

Favorite TV Show: She and I are always watching Edo-period dramas together.

Favorite Book: I see her with manga all the time.

Strong Points: She's an eternal optimist, and she makes friends easily.

One Last Word: She's a big sister that a girl can always rely on.

NOT TOO LONG AGO, I WAS AN UPPITY, BRATTY MIDDLE-SCHOOL KID.

A TRUE, HOPELESS IDIOT.

AND I WAS A GOD!!

I WASN'T TIED DOWN TO ANY-BODY OR ANY-THING!

#06 YOU'VE GOT MAIL

I...

WHEN I FELL IN LOVE WITH TSUKA-MOTO TENMA!

BUT ONE WOMAN CHANGED ALL THAT.

A CHALLENGE LETTER?

CHALLENGE

I'VE NEVER LOVED FROM AFAR. I HAVE NO IDEA WHAT TO DO.

BUT HOW CAN I LET HER KNOW?

KACHAK
ガチャ

Harima Kenji: Late.

OH, HIM!

TENNŌJI NOBORU?

......

IS THIS SOME KIND OF JOKE?

HE WROTE THE KANJI WRONG.

I MEAN, WHO SENDS A LETTER NOWADAYS?

THAT'S THE ANSWER!!

RIPP

NO, JUST THE OPPOSITE!

BECAUSE IT'S A LETTER IT HAS A GREATER IMPACT!

Harima Kenji: *Makes His Move.*

I'LL JUST TAKE A NAP HERE ON THE ROOF...

SHE'LL MEET ME AT 4 P.M. BEHIND THE GYM.

TAKE THIS!

THE MOST PERFECT

LOVE LETTER

THE WORLD HAS EVER SEEN!!

TSUKAMOTO

スッ

SWIPP

THE NEXT DAY NEAR THE SCHOOL ENTRANCE...

TSUKAMOTO

THIS IS IT! TENMA-CHAN'S SHOE LOCKER!

I... UM...

I, UM....!

ハウ WHSSH

• • •
• • •
• • •

HARIMA-KUN...

TENMA-CHAN! SHE'S ALREADY WAITING!

HM...

OKAY, IT'S ALMOST TIME...

THIS'LL BE GREAT!

♪♪

WHO THE...

WAIT... I'VE SEEN HIM SOMEWHERE...

THAT'S IT! IT'S THE JERK WHO SENT ME THE CHALLENGE!!

WHAT WAS HIS NAME... TENNŌJI NOBORU OR SOMETHING LIKE THAT?

WAS HIS CHALLENGE FOR EXACTLY THE SAME TIME AND PLACE AS MY PROMISE TO TENMA-CHAN?

DAMMIT! I'D LIKE TO TAKE HIM ON, BUT NOW I CAN'T!

YOU'RE GOING TO SPEND THE REST OF YOUR LIFE IN THE HOSPITAL!

HARIMA... YOU WON'T GET AWAY WITH JUST TWO OR THREE CRACKED RIBS!

I'LL JUST BORROW IT A MINUTE!

AH?! N-NOOO!!

EH? I'M WAITING FOR SOMEONE.

HELLO? MISS?

I'VE NOTICED YOU'VE BEEN HERE FOR A WHILE. WHAT ARE YOU DOING?

SMILE

Y-YEAH...

HOOOH? A LETTER, IS IT?

THE BIG BEAST!!

THAT CREEP! WHERE'D HE GET THE NERVE TO TALK TO HER!

W-WAIT!!

NOW WHAT'S THIS HERE? COULD IT BE A *POEM*?!

"THANK YOU,"
ARE THE WORDS I WANT TO CONVEY.
THE FIRST WORDS TO SAY
TO A MOTHER AND FATHER.
*"THANK YOU FOR RAISING
SOMEONE SO SWEET."*
I CAN ONLY SAY,
*"THANK YOU, FROM THE BOTTOM
OF MY HEART."*

STOP! PLEASE! STOP!

EH?

: : : :

IS THAT WHAT YOU THINK OF IT...?

THE ONLY THING I WANNA DO NOW IS GET OUT THERE AND BASH THAT GUY!

GWA HA HA HA!!

WHO COULD FIGURE THAT POEM OUT?! AND WHAT GOOD'S A VERSE THAT MAKES YOU LAUGH?

IT'S TOO BAD HE NEVER SIGNED IT!

...ARE THE WRITER'S TRUE FEELINGS.

AND... THINK THE FEELING OF LOVE IN THIS LETTER...

...BUT AT TIMES LIKE THIS, I TRY MY BEST TO FEEL WHAT THE WRITER FEELS.

I KNOW I'M NOT VERY SMART...

I CAN'T HELP BUT LOVE THIS POEM!

...THIS IS THE HAPPIEST I'VE EVER FELT!

EVER SINCE I FELL FOR TENMA-CHAN...

WHAT IS HE TRYING TO PULL?!

YOU'RE THE ONE WHO NOBODY CAN FIGURE OUT!

I WANT TO GO OUT THERE, BUT I JUST CAN'T!

ACTUALLY, *I'M* THE ONE WHO WROTE IT.

I LOVE YOU!!

THANK YOU!

BUT...I'M IN LOVE WITH SOMEBODY ELSE.

SHKK

06 . . . . Fin.

IF IT'S JUST A DATE... SURE, I'LL GO.

Tsukamoto Tenma introduces...

SAWA CHIKA E RI
沢近愛理

STATS:

Height: 165 cm (5' 5")... or somewhere around there.

Favorite Thing: She once told me it was the zoo.

Least Favorite Thing: I think it's kanji and cooking.

Special Talent: She's a genius who can master just about anything! I'm sooo jealous!

Weak Points: She may not look it, but she can be even sadder than I get.

Notes: Her father's British and her mother's Japanese, so she's mixed race. She's now back in Japan from living in England. She was raised with a silver spoon in her mouth.

One Last Word: Her language may be a little rough, but really she's a nice girl, I'm sure of it!

TIME, HUH? I WONDER IF THERE'S ANY WAY I CAN GET KARASUMA-KUN TO SPEND MORE TIME WITH ME...

ヒラ
FLUTTER
FLUTTER
ヒラ

AH! A BUTTER-FLY!

An overpass on the way to school...

IS THERE ANY PLACE OTHER THAN SCHOOL I CAN BE WITH HER?

AH! A BUTTER-FLY!

むう?! HMM...

ト゛ッ
ト゛ッ
ト゛ッ

GRMM

ト゛ッ

GRMM

ト゛ッ

GRMM

I GOTTA GET MORE CHANCES TO SPEND TIME WITH TENMA-CHAN!

MM...?

ちりん
ちりん

CHING CHING

HM...?

YEP!

WE HAVE NICE WEATHER AGAIN TODAY, DON'T WE, TSUKAMOTO-SAN?

OH! YOU'RE RIGHT, HUH?

WE HAVE NICE WEATHER AGAIN TODAY, DON'T WE, HARIMA-SAN?

THAT'S IT!!!

DM DM DM DM

THIS COULD WORK!!

TMP

キッ！

SKEEK

THERE HE IS! RIGHT! NOW I'LL JUST DO THE MOST NATURAL OF GREETINGS...

ちりん ちりん
CHING CHING

EH?!

ちりん ちりん
CHING CHING

SHOOOM

KARASUMA-KUN, GOOD MOR—

...THE POWER OF LOVE!!

AH! IT'S TENMA-CHAN! AND SHE HAS A BIKE EVEN BEFORE I ASKED HER TO RIDE WITH ME! THAT MUST BE...

SKEEK

WAIT UP, KARASUMA-KUN!!

KARASUMA-KUN?! OH, NO! WAIT!

HE'S SO FAST!!

BUT HE'S JUST RIDING A NORMAL MAMA-CHARI, ISN'T HE?!

SHNNK SHNNK SHNNK

Tsukamoto Tenma: Going All Out!

WHA—?!

Y-YO, TENMA-CHAN! THIS IS SUCH A COINCI- DENCE—

Yagami-saka Hill on the way to school...

YAAH! WAIT UP, TENMA-CHAN!!

EVEN IF SHE'S TRYING TO DIET, SHE'S RIDING WAY TOO HARD. WHAT A WASTE OF BODY POWER!

WHAT'S GOING ON? WHY IS SHE SUDDENLY RIDING SO HARD?

CHNNK
CHNNK
CHNNK

うおお— HYAAA!

HM?

TSK!

GOOD MORNING, SAWACHIKA- SAN.

しゃ SHHHH

GOOD MORNING! KARASUMA-KUN! ♥

I WORKED SO HARD ON MY HAIR THIS MORNING, IT'D BE A SHAME NOT TO SHOW IT OFF TO THE GUYS!

...しゃ SHHH

SHUUUM

AWW! HE COULD HAVE LOOKED AT MY HAIR A LITTLE LONGER!

HE'S FAST!!

AND HE GOES UP SHISSHIN-SAKA HILL WITHOUT A HINT OF STRAIN.

HEY, THAT'S...

↑ Sawachika misread Yagami-saka Hill as Shisshin-saka Hill.

And at school...

...and completely wasted the time they could have spent with the object of their affections.

The exhausted pair fell quickly asleep...

A completely unfazed Karasuma.

07 . . . . Fin.

OH, NO! THE REFRIGERATOR AT HOME IS COMPLETELY EMPTY!

SQEE

AH!

WHAT'S UP?

The ladies' room after school...

EH? OH, YEAH. WELL...

COOKING? YOU? I NEVER EXPECTED THAT!

I'M EXPECTING YAKUMO TO COOK IT.

I SHOULD LEAVE SCHOOL AS SOON AS POSSIBLE AND PICK UP GROCERIES.

KREE

WHAT SHOULD I HAVE FOR DINNER?

#08   THE GREAT ESCAPE

HM...

YOU KNOW, YOU LOOK A LOT LIKE A SPOILED RICH GIRL.

HUH? ...YOU THINK SO?

I-IT'S KARASUMA-KUN!

Reflexively...

ZWIP

THE MINUTE A GIRL STOPS HERSELF FROM LEAVING, IT'S SO HARD TO LEAVE AGAIN.

OH, HECK!

I'M SO STUPID!

IS IT THAT I'M UPTIGHT ABOUT BEING SEEN LEAVING THE LADIES ROOM?

HUH? WHY AM I HIDING?!

...NO. I DON'T REALLY GET IT MY-SELF, BUT MORE IM-PORTANTLY...

UM... YOU'RE BLOCK-ING THE DOOR.

TSUKAMOTO-SAN...

OHHHH

WHAT'LL I DO?!

TREMBLE

IT'S JUST A BATHROOM! THAT'S ALL!!

TREMBLE

IT TAKES SOME NERVE TO STAND OUTSIDE THE LADIES' RESTROOM CASUALLY CHATTING.

BUT THAT'S WHAT I LOVE ABOUT HIM!

AWW! KARASUMA-KUN, YOU BIG DUMMY!

HE'S STILL THERE.

A BATTLE OF WILLS!

SO THAT'S WHAT THIS IS.

ㄴ—— STARE ‥‥

So...

RIGHT! YOU'LL SEE HOW MUCH I CAN TAKE!!

A HALLWAY CHAT CAN'T TAKE MORE THAN 10 MINUTES TOPS!

I'LL JUST CONSIDER THIS A TEST.

OKAY THEN! YOU'LL SEE JUST HOW STRONG-MINDED A WOMAN CAN BE!

COME TO THINK OF IT, A PERSON HAS TO ENDURE A LOT IN LOVE, TOO!

HE'S TAKEN TO READING OUT THERE!

AND IT LOOKS LIKE A NOVEL.

HOW BRIGHT THE SUN IS OUT HERE!

THAT'S 30 MINUTES I'VE HELD OUT FOR!

TIME TO LEAVE!

KREEE

TSUKA-MOTO, ARE YOU *STILL* IN THE BATH-ROOM?

NOT POSSIBLE, RIGHT?

KREE

I TAKE THREE STEPS, AND SHE'S GONE.

GACHAK

MISSION NO. 2! LEAVING IN DISGUISE!

Toilet Paper.

IT ISN'T LIKE I HAVE A WHOLE LOT OF OPTIONS! AS LONG AS I KNOW WHAT I'M DOING, IT DOESN'T MATTER IF NOBODY ELSE DOES!

MUMBLE MUMBLE

E Y A A H?!

WHAA–?!

HOW'D YOU KNOW?

I'M GOING HOME. OKAY, TSUKAMOTO?

Changing her voice.

AH, YOUR TIMING IS PERFECT!

GUESS WHO!

FLY !!!

VWUUM

PLAN NO. 3! I'LL THROW THIS MOP TO DRAW HIS ATTENTION AWAY, AND THEN MAKE MY MOVE!

ONE...

TWO...

NOW I CAN'T *EVER* LEAVE!

NO THOUGHTS ABOUT HARIMA AT ALL?

CALL THE POLICES

WHAT HAPPENED?

WHAAH! WHY? WHY DOES THIS HAPPEN TO ME?!

GONK

PWOOO

Tsukamoto Tenma: No Self-Control.

IT COULD WORK!!

Rubber suction-cup plunger.

MIKOTO-CHAN GAVE UP ON ME AND WENT HOME. I'M A WOMAN WARRIOR STANDING ALONE ON THE BATTLEFIELD...

SHIPOH

SHIPOH

SORRY, HARIMA-KUN! I'LL APOLOGIZE TO YOU LATER!

AWW, NOTHING GOES RIGHT FOR ME!

SHOMP

GRNN GRNN

HUH? IT WON'T COME OFF!

CHA-PPO

LEFT SIDE, SET!!

RIGHT SIDE, SET!!

CHA-PPO

20 MINUTES LATER...

08 . . . . Fin.

BUY ME LUNCH AND I'LL FORGET THAT YOU GOT HERE LATE.

Sawachika Eri introduces...

SU Ô MI KOTO
周防美琴

STATS:

Height: 170 cm (5' 7") maybe? Yeah, about that.

Favorite Thing: She says it's cooking and singing.

Least Favorite Thing: Her father, I hear. But in a different way than me with my father.

Special Talent: Every sport around, martial arts, drinks like a fish, and is so much more athletic than I am.

Childhood Dream: To become a nurse. I'm kidding about that, of course.

One Last Word: I'm so jealous of her free-flowing black hair, but I think she should get a more feminine cut. What a waste!

♯09 THE GIRL WHO KNEW LITTLE

⋯⋯⋯⋯⋯⋯

B-
BMP
B-
BMP

FIDGET
FIDGET

IT'S BEEN SO LONG SINCE WE WERE LAST TOGETHER.

I JUST WANT TO ASK... TREAT ME GENTLY, OKAY?

U-UM...

THAT?

AH! NO! I JUST... I MEAN... THAT.

EH!?

CHK

SHE SAW ME!!

HEY NEE-CHAN, WHO'RE YOU TALKING TO?

Her Younger Sister's Name: Tsukamoto Yakumo.

The day of the measurements check at school...

KARASUMA-KUN WILL GET A MEASUREMENTS CHECK TOO, HUH?

I WONDER...

GYAAH!!

I WANNA KNOW! I WANNA KNOW! IT'S LIKE I'M THE ONLY ONE IN THE WORLD WHO DOESN'T KNOW KARASUMA-KUN'S DATA!

WHAFF WHAFF

WHAT'S HIS HEIGHT? A HUNDRED SEVENTY... ONE? TWO?
(5' 7" OR 5' 8")

HIS WEIGHT SEEMS LIKE IT'D BE PRETTY LIGHT... HE GIVES A LIMBER KIND OF IMPRESSION.

BUT I CAN NEVER REALLY GUESS AT A GUY'S WEIGHT.

HMM...

HEY! ABOUT TODAY...

POP

HEY, TSUKA–

EH?! I-I'M SORRY!!

COME ON! WHY DO YOU LIKE APOLOGIZING SO MUCH?!

WAIT A MINUTE! WHAT EXACTLY ARE YOU SORRY FOR?

HEY!

BUT HIS CHEST SIZE IS PROBABLY BIGGER THAN MINE.

IT MAKES ME A LITTLE MAD AND A LITTLE DEPRESSED.

ALL THE GUYS ARE STRANGELY NERVOUS.

OH, THEY'RE PROBABLY ALL WORKED UP WITH NASTY LITTLE THOUGHTS OVER THE MEASUREMENT CHECK TODAY.

IF THEY'RE SO WORKED UP TO SEE THAT KIND OF THING, THEY SHOULD JUST BECOME DOCTORS OR NURSEMAIDS.

BUT ISN'T IT A LITTLE CREEPY? BOYS SUDDENLY MADE USELESS BY THEIR OWN IMAGINATIONS?

Sawachika Eri: *Born in Tokyo.*

"IF THEY'RE SO WORKED UP, THEY SHOULD JUST BECOME DOCTORS..."

THEN MAYBE A NURSE...?

ALL I'M SAYING IS THE BOYS AREN'T PUTTING ANY REAL EFFORT INTO WHAT THEY WISH FOR!

ARE YOU SOME KIND OF IDIOT?!

I'VE BEEN WONDERING THAT FOR A WHILE.

CORRECTION. THE WORD IS NOT "NURSE-MAIDS," BUT "NURSES." NURSEMAID IS SOMETHING ELSE ENTIRELY.

AHHH! DON'T ASK ME!

DOESN'T IT SEEM AS THOUGH SHE SUDDENLY SETTLED ON A COURSE OF ACTION?

IT COULD WORK!

JUST BECOME A NURSE!!

IT SOUNDED LIKE SHE WAS SERIOUS!

KNOWING HER...

Tsukamoto Tenma: *Completely Illogical.*

YOU DON'T THINK THAT MAYBE SHE...

ARE YOU SURE?

I STILL HAVE AN ODD, OMINOUS FEELING.

R-REALLY? THAT'S GOOD TO HEAR!

AH...

NO! NO! IT ISN'T A COURSE OF ACTION!

THERE'S SOMETHING I GOTTA DO, SO I'LL SEE YOU!

GREAT! A COMPLETE TRANSFOR-MATION!!

THAT LITTLE IDIOT!!

FOR WHAT PUR-POSE?

THAT ISN'T THE PROB-LEM!

THEY'LL KNOW IT'S HER FROM HER HAIR STYLE!

MURMUR   MURMUR

DOOOM

YOU'RE KIDDING!!

MIKOTO IS CORRECT. INTERFERENCE WOULD BE ILL-ADVISED.

WE DON'T! WE JUST LET HER BE. I SHOULD SAY, WE WATCH WHAT HAPPENS.

HOWEVER, I INTEND TO END THIS WHEN THE TIME IS RIGHT.

GWIP

AH HA HA HA! I'LL BET ANYTHING SHE'S WRITING "TSUKAMOTO" ON IT!

NOTICE THE JOY WITH WHICH SHE PENS HER NAME ON HER BADGE.

HOW DO WE STOP HER?!

I HAVEN'T DONE THIS SINCE GRADE SCHOOL!

OH?

I HAVE A FEELING I KNOW WHAT SHE'S UP TO...

IT TAKES A WEIRDO TO KNOW A WEIRDO?

SORRY TO KEEP YOU WAITING!!!

ば TA-DAH ん

ALL RIGHT!! I GOT MYSELF A SET OF KARASUMA-KUN'S MEASUREMENTS!

I'M A SUDDEN TRANSFER. DR. HARIMA. PLEASED TO MEET YOU.

THE SAME GOES FOR ME. SORRY FOR MY LATE ARRIVAL.

IT IS SO NICE TO BE WORKING WITH YOU, DOCTOR!

And not too long afterward, the measurement checks for the day were canceled.

For some reason or other...

#09 ......Fin.

BE CALM.
NOTHING IS
IMPOSSIBLE
FOR YOU.

Suô Mikoto
introduces . . .

TAKA   NO   AKIRA
高野　晶

STATS:

Height: 166 cm (5' 5") or thereabouts, I think.

Favorite Thing: Economizing

Least Favorite Thing: Falling into debt, they say.

Favorite Word: Persevere . . . I think.

Hobby: Gunpura . . . what in the world is that?

Special Talent: The koto and Japanese dance.
You know that's gotta be a joke, right?

Notes: I don't know the reason for it, but she's
loaded down with part-time jobs.

One Last Word: The girl's getting good grades.
She's got a lot of stuff going on that we don't
have a clue about.

#10 LA BELLE NOISEUSE

YES, LET'S DO THAT.

I-I'M PAIRED WITH KARASUMA-KUN?!

L-LET'S TRY TO DO OUR BEST, OKAY?

WHEN I LOOK INTO KARASUMA-KUN'S EYES...

GLIMPSE

B-BUT...

HOW'RE YOU GONNA DO YOUR BEST WHEN YOU'RE HIDING YOUR FACE? KARASUMA-KUN CAN'T DRAW YOU.

もじ もじ

MUMBLE MUMBLE

YET SOMEHOW IT MAKES IT EASIER FOR KARASUMA-KUN TO DRAW.

AND HERE *WE* ARE, A GROUP OF GIRLS!

SHE HASN'T MOVED AN INCH IN A WHILE NOW. DOES SHE EVEN *WANT* TO DO THIS?

SKRCH SKRCH スラ スラ

フキン キン

カチク KACHIK

ガチク GACHIK

ZANNG

— 84 —

KARASUMA-KUN IS LOOKING AT ME KARASUMA-KUN IS LOOKING AT ME KARASUMA-KUN IS LOOKING AT ME KARASUMA-KUN IS LOOKING AT ME SUMA-KUN IS LOOKING AT ME KARASUMA-KUN IS LOOKING AT ME KARASUMA-KUN IS LOOKIN G AT ME KARASUMA-KUN IS LOOKING AT ME KARASUMA-KUN IS LOOKI AT ME KARASUMA-KUN IS LOOKING AT ME LOOKING AT ME KARASUMA-KUN IS LOOK AT ME KARASUMA-KUN IS LOOKING AT ME KARASUMA-KUN IS LOOKING AT ME KARAS ME KARASUMA-KUN IS LOOKING AT ME LOOKING AT ME KARASUMA-KUN IS LOOK KU-N IS LOOKING AT ME KARASUMA-KUN IS LOOKING AT ME KARAS AT ME KARASUMA-KUN IS LOOKING AT ME KARASUMA-KUN IS LOOKING AT ME KARAS AT ME KARASUMA-KUN IS LOOKING AT ME LOOKING AT ME KARASUMA-KUN IS LOOK KUN IS LOOKING AT ME KARASUMA-KUN IS LOOKING AT ME KARASUMA-KUN IS LOOKING AT ME KAR ME KARASUMA-KUN

HEY, WAIT! I WANT HIM TO WATCH THE FUTURE ME, TOO! JUST STAY LIKE THIS! STAY LIKE THIS FOREVER!

WATCH ME! WATCH ME ENOUGH FOR A WHOLE LIFE'S WORTH OF WATCHING!!

SURE. SEE YOU WHEN YOU'RE BACK.

KARASUMA-KUN! UM ... I HAVE TO ... UM ... WHAT ... BATHROOM! AH! I MEAN ... NO, I ...

SHUDDER

AH?!

TMP TMP TMP TMP TMP

OH, HONESTLY!!

...AND I NEVER DID MY HAIR!!

THIS MORNING I SLEPT IN A LITTLE ...

WHOOSH

Tsukamoto Tenma: *In Bliss.*

I KNOW! I CAN CUT IT TO A SHORT-HAIR LOOK!

THAT WON'T WORK! I'M TOO CLUMSY TO CUT MY OWN HAIR.

IT ISN'T GETTING ANY BETTER!

WAAH! WHY DID THIS HAVE TO HAPPEN TODAY? YAKUMO! WAKE ME UP AT THE RIGHT TIME!!

It's always someone else's fault.

Awwww!

IT IS!! FRIZZ AND SPLIT ENDS!

SHSS SHSS

IT'S NO PROBLEM.

I'M REALLY SORRY!

I MADE YOU WAIT SO LONG.

I GUESS I CAN MANAGE WITH THIS.

HE'S GOT IT SO WRONG!!

BESIDES, HOLDING IT IN IS BAD FOR YOUR HEALTH.

NO, I REALLY DID IT FOR ME...

NO! WHAT ARE YOU SAYING?! YOU BIG DUMMY! KARASUMA-KUN, YOU'RE SO DUMB! I DID IT FOR YOU!

Tsukamoto Tenma: A *Victim of Static Electricity.*

STARE

ちら、

GLIMPSE

I'LL JUST DO A NORMAL DRAWING.

I'D BETTER STOP THINKING LIKE THIS.

IF I WANT TO PLACE KARASUMA-KUN'S IMAGE ON PAPER, OUR GAZES MUST NATURALLY MEET AND INTERTWINE.

Gross overstatement. ♪

I'M SO NERVOUS, I HAVEN'T BEEN ABLE TO LOOK AT HIM.

W-WHAT'LL I DO?

THERE! ♥ I DID IT!

SHFF SHFF

HMMM

IF I DRAW HIM WITH MY EYES SLIGHTLY OUT OF FOCUS ...

Y-YES, THAT'S IT.

— 87 —

THAT ISN'T TRUE!!

I DON'T KNOW KARASUMA-KUN'S FACE AT ALL ANY MORE!

WHAT'LL I DO? WHAT'LL I DO?

THAT'S AWFUL!

WAIT JUST ONE SECOND! AM I REALLY SAYING THAT I DON'T KNOW KARASUMA-KUN'S FACE?

"DON'T KNOW"?

...LOSE SIGHT OF HIM!!

I WILL NEVER...

ZIT

I CAN JUST CLOSE MY EYES, AND...

HIS IMAGE BURNED INTO MY RETINAS!

I KNOW IT!

SNAP!

GLANCE

LOOK AT TSUKA-MOTO-SAN. SHE'S ON TOP OF THE WORLD!

AT LEAST *DRAW* LIKE A NORMAL PERSON, OKAY?

ALL RIGHT, EVERYONE! TURN IN YOUR SKETCHES.

DINNNG DONNNG

キーン コーン カーン

KLAP KLAP

SHE WAS DRAWING WITH HER EYES CLOSED! WHAT'S WITH THIS GIRL?

NOPE! IT'S JUST THAT EVERY SO OFTEN I COME UP WITH A GOOD PICTURE.

HEY, THAT'S A SURPRISE! YOU'RE NOT A BAD ARTIST, TSUKAMOTO. YOU BEEN PRACTICING?

WHAT'S THAT SUPPOSED TO MEAN?

Sawachika Eri: *Jealousy.*

AAH! I'VE BEEN CAUGHT!

BUT HOW'D YOU DRAW HIM AT AN ANGLE WITH HIM LOOKING AT YOU?

WHAT STYLE DID YOU DRAW ME IN?

KARA-SUMA-KUN...

SAWA-CHIKA! LUNCH IN THE CAFETERIA TODAY?

WOULD THAT MEAN THAT HE THOUGHT THE REAL ME WAS CUTE? WELL, IT *MAY* NOT MEAN THAT...

MAYBE HE DREW A REALLY CUTE PICTURE OF ME...

BUT THAT'S HOW I'D TAKE IT!

NOW...

OKAY, THEN I'LL SUBMIT MINE RIGHT AFTER KARASUMA-KUN SUBMITS HIS.

THEN I'LL TAKE JUST A QUICK GLANCE.

I REALLY WANT TO KNOW!

Ukiyo-e.

10 .... Fin.

THERE'S SOMEBODY STILL IN HERE!!

ガチャ!! GACHANK

WHA–?

THIS SEEMS TO HAPPEN TO ME A LOT.

IS IT IN MY BLOOD?

IT'S NO GOOD. I DON'T THINK I CAN GET DOWN FROM HERE.

Gym Storeroom, 2nd Floor...

#11 THE TOWERING INFERNO

Tsukamoto Tenma is the type of girl who doesn't quite understand the situation until it becomes so serious that she can't ignore it.

In short, she's pretty dim.

O-OH, WELL. IT SHOULD BE OKAY.

ONCE CLUB ACTIVITIES BEGIN, SOMEBODY WILL COME BY.

AFTER A LONG TIME

I HAVE TO STOP THIS!

I HAVE TO BE OPTIMISTIC! I CAN PUT THIS SITUATION TO USE TO HELP ME SOMEHOW!

GAMPH

RIGHT! IT'S AN EXPERIENCE! IT ISN'T LIKE MY LIFE IS IN DANGER. YEAH, THAT'S HOW TO SEE IT!

ROLL!

I CAN'T EVEN DO HOMEWORK. I'LL HAVE TO EXPLAIN WHY TOMORROW.

"I WAS LOCKED UP, AND I WASN'T ABLE TO DO IT." MAYBE THAT'LL WORK.

AWWW! THERE'S A TV PROGRAM I REALLY WANTED TO SEE!

I WONDER IF YAKUMO IS RECORDING IT FOR ME.

WAAAH!

ALL OF THE CLUBS HAVE THE DAY OFF!!

I'LL THINK OF THIS AS HAVING JUST ARRIVED ASHORE ON A DESERT ISLAND. IMAGINE THIS AS AN EXTREME SITUATION. RIGHT! THIS IS A TEST FOR ME! THIS IS A CHANCE TO PROVE MY PRESENCE OF MIND!

グ! GRMP

I WAS *JOKING* ABOUT FINDING FOOD.

...IT'S A BUN.

AND IT'S PRETTY NEW.

FIRST ORDER OF BUSINESS IS TO FIND FOOD.

ゴゾ ゴゾ RUSTLE RUSTLE

WOW! THINKING LIKE GOT ME ALL EXCITED!

→ Getting into it.

I'M THE MOST WEAK-WILLED PERSON IN THE WORLD!

もぐ もぐ MUNCH MUNCH

NO! NO WAY!! I DON'T CARE HOW GOOD IT LOOKS, EATING THIS WOULD BE JUST TOO DANGEROU—

GROWL

つつつ

BUT COME TO THINK OF IT, I *AM* KINDA HUNGRY. I WONDER IF IT'S OKAY IF I EAT THIS?

I'D RATHER NOT IF IT'S GOT SOME WEIRD FILLING.

....

!?

GAK! "FLAMING HOT CURRY BUN"?!

NO WONDER! I AM *SO* BAD WITH SPICY FOODS! AW, MAN!!

KAFF! KAFF! KAFF!

IT'S HOT!! IT'S TOO SPICY!

BUT WHAT'LL I DO? THE PLUMBING DOESN'T COME UP HERE! NOW I'M IN A *REAL* BATTLE FOR SURVIVAL!

GULP! I'M GETTING THIRSTY. I WANT WATER!

YOU DUMB—!!

KRIKK

HUH? HOW AM I SUP-POSED TO MAKE THIS WORK? THERE'S NO SWITCH...

UNNNG! THIS IS BEGINNING TO TICK ME OFF!!

NGH! UFF! COME ON, WORK! YOU LITTLE—

AH! I KNOW! I CAN USE THE SPRINKLER SYSTEM!

THERE *IS* ACCESS TO WATER UP HERE!

— 94 —

AHHH! NOW I KNOW WHAT IT FEELS LIKE TO BE SHIPWRECKED. YUP, I SURE DO!

WOW! THIS FEELS SO GOOD! WATER! I MADE WATER!

I OPENED THE PIPE!

I DID IT! IT'S WORKING!

I WONDER WHAT I'D THINK IF I COULDN'T EVER GET OUT OF HERE.

....

WHY DON'T I EVER REALIZE THE OBVIOUS THINGS LIKE THAT? IT'S A MYSTERY.

I DON'T HAVE A CHANGE OF CLOTHES OR A TOWEL.

I THINK I'D BE A LITTLE MORE AT EASE KNOWING MY FATE...

...BUT I KNOW I'D BE LONELY.

I WONDER WHAT KARASUMA-KUN IS DOING RIGHT NOW.

むくり

SHLIPP

YOU WERE SLEEPING HERE? THEN I'M SORRY I MADE SO MUCH NOISE!

EH? OH!

BOW BOW

IT'S HARD TO SLEEP.

ON THESE MATS.

GLOOB

.....GLOOB?

B-BUT...

KARASUMA-KUN!! YOU CAME HERE TO SAVE ME?!

TMP

TSUKAMOTO-SAN IS
PRETTY AMAZING.

Actually,
that was
Karasuma-
kun's
bun.

MUNCH
MUNCH

ZOOOM

*I AM SO
EMBARRASSED!!!*

11 . . . . Fin.

IT'S GETTING REALLY LATE! YAKUMO IS GONNA BE MAD AT ME.

#12 UNFORGIVEN

MAYBE I'LL JUST TAKE THE SHORTCUT THROUGH THE WOODS...

OKAY, YAKUMO! YOUR BIG SISTER WILL KEEP HER PROMISE TO YOU!

"DO YOU KNOW WHAT YOU'RE SAYING?"

"THOSE GUYS ARE MUCH MORE SCARY THAN ANY BEAR!"

"NEE-CHAN, DON'T EVER TAKE THE PATH THROUGH THE WOODS."

BUT COME TO THINK OF IT, YAKUMO SAID...

"WHY NOT?"

"THEY SAY THERE'S A RAPIST STALKING THE WOODS."

"JUST THAT? I THOUGHT IT'D BE A BEAR OR SOMETHING."

IT'S KARA-SUMA-KUN!!

AH!

NOW TO THE PATH!

SWITCH ON!

TMP

SHKK

TSUKAMOTO-SAN! I'LL PROTECT YOU!

Rapist.

KARASUMA-KUN!

YOU'D DO THAT FOR ME?

Me.

KARASUMA-KUN! ♡ → STANDING UP TO THE BEAST WITH HIS BARE HANDS!

TH- THAT'S IT!!

I COULD USE THIS OPPORTUNITY TO DEEPEN OUR LOVE!

THIS IS MY CHANCE! FIRST, I MUST FOLLOW HER. THEN TENMA-CHAN WILL SOON BE THREATENED BY THE RAPIST!

THAT IS WHEN I WILL STEP IN AND SAVE HER! THEN WILL SPROUT THE SEEDS OF LOVE!!

KLNCH

IT'S PERFECT! THIS IS THE START OF A LOVE STORY SO WONDERFUL, IT SCARES EVEN ME!

AWW, TENMA-CHAN! THIS PATH THROUGH THE WOODS IS SUCH A DANGEROUS PLACE FOR YOUNG GIRLS TO WALK. I CAN'T SIMPLY STAND BY!

I'M GLAD I FOLLOWED YOU HERE.

TSK!

HOWEVER... HUMPH! ANYONE CAN SEE WHAT'S COMING. JUST AS MY PLAN IS COMING TO FRUITION...

I'M SURE THAT SOMEBODY WILL MISTAKE ME FOR THE RAPIST AND I'LL BE ARRESTED.

THAT'S WHAT'LL REALLY HAPPEN.

THAT'S PROBABLY JUST WHAT HE IS HOPING FOR, BUT...

GLEEM

I CAN FIGURE OUT WHAT'S GOING TO HAPPEN EVEN WHEN THE PLOT IS WRITTEN BY AN A-LIST SCREENWRITER!

SOMEONE LIKE UCHIDATE MAKIKO!

TODAY, YOU'LL FIND THAT SOMETHING IS DIFFERENT ABOUT ME!

YES...

HE UNDER-ESTIMATES ME!

MY POLICE OFFICER DISGUISE IS PERFECT!

スキャ!

SKTCH!

KAWW KAWW

WHAT'LL I DO? I'VE EVEN LOST SIGHT OF KARASUMA-KUN!

IF THE RAPIST WERE TO ATTACK ME NOW...

I'VE LOST MY WAY!!

THIS LOOKS LIKE ONE POOR, TROUBLED HIGH SCHOOL COED.

THERE'S NO ONE AROUND. THIS MAY BE PERFECT!

HEHN...

SHIKK

オ—
オ—

TREMBLE

TREMBLE

EH?!

PRETTY SOON, I'LL FREE IT FROM ALL THOSE AWFUL CLOTHES!

THAT'S SOME BODY YOU GOT THERE, GIRL!

RAPE IS A *CRIME*, MISTER.

HWOOOO

JUSTICE IS DONE!!

I-IT WORKED PERFECTLY! TENMA-CHAN HAS NOW, UNDOUBTEDLY...

...*COMPLETELY FALLEN IN LOVE WITH ME!*

ARE YOU ALL RIGHT?

Y-YES, I AM! YOU SAVED ME! I...UM...

OHHHH,

NOOOO!!!

THANK YOU SO MUCH, MR. POLICEMAN!!

BOW

Like she trusts him absolutely.

WHAT WONDER- FUL WORK YOU DO.

H-HOW THICK CAN A GIRL GET?! YES, I AM A POLICEMAN AT THIS MOMENT, BUT IF I SIMPLY TAKE OFF THE HAT, SHE CAN'T HELP BUT REALIZE THAT I'M HARIMA!

BUT EVEN SO, I THINK IT'S SO GREAT THAT YOU'D GO OUT OF YOUR WAY TO HELP ME, A COMPLETE STRANGER!

YEAH...

JUST DOING MY JOB, MA'AM!

YES, SIR! AND THANK YOU SO MUCH!

PLEASE TAKE BETTER CARE OF YOURSELF, TSUKAMOTO-SAN.

BUT MY DUTY IS FINISHED HERE.

OH, IT DOESN'T MATTER.

?

HOW DID HE KNOW MY NAME?

12 . . . . Fin.

Q.E.D.

Takano Akira introduces...

OSA KA BE ITO KO
刑部絃子

STATS:

Height: 168 cm (5' 6")

Favorite Thing: Planck's Constant

Least Favorite Thing: Extensions of classtime

Favorite Food: Functional foods

Hobby: She admires mechanisms and reportedly has a large collection of model guns.

Special Talent: Can recite the answer to a multiplication of any two five-digit numbers in under three seconds.

One Last Word: In my opinion, she should display more interest in teaching. Her education methods are impeccable.

#13 BROKEN ARROW

...ABOUT MY LOVE LETTER TO KARASUMA-KUN?

WHAT'LL I DO...

SIGH!

I WANT A *WAY* TO GIVE HIM THE MESSAGE THAT WILL LEAVE AN IMPRESSION.

I FIGURED OUT EARLIER THAT I HAVE NO TALENT FOR WRITING...

SO I HAVE TO COME UP WITH SOMETHING ELSE...

I JUST WANTED TO BE SURE YOU KNEW IT WAS GOING TO START...

EH?! IT'S TIME ALREADY?!

She's been lost in thought ever since she got home.

CAN'T YOU TELL JUST BY LOOKING?! HONESTLY!

I'M SORRY.

SHORT ON SLEEP?

I'M LONG ON WORRIES!!

The next morning...

UM, NEE-CHAN?

I'M STILL NOT SURE WHAT YOU'RE PLANNING, BUT...

THAT'S TOP SECRET! I'LL NEVER TELL A USE-LESS LITTLE SISTER WHO CAN'T EVEN SEE WHEN HER ELDERS ARE WORRIED!

HUH...? WH-WHAT COULD WORK?

HA HA HA HA

NOW, MY BATH AWAITS!!

HM! ONE SENSES IT MOST PALPABLY!

THAT BOW IS REALLY GETTING IN THE WAY.

YAKUMO-DONO, ONE WILL GRACIOUSLY REFRAIN FROM YOUR BOUNTIFUL BREAKFAST!

TMP

FORTH!!

SHK SHK SHK SHK SHK

TALK ABOUT WORRIES...

Runs the way samurai run.

JUST YOU WAIT! YOU'LL GET A BIG SURPRISE, YAKUMO!

HUH? YOU MEAN YOU WANT TO SUR-PRISE ME MORE?!

JUST WHAT DO YOU INTEND TO DO?

VWIP

WE'RE READY FOR ANYTHING!

LISTEN, WE'RE GETTIN' TOGETHER TONIGHT.

I WANT SOME COFFEE.

BOSS COFFEE IS THE ONLY ONE FOR A MAN!

Karasuma-kun even wears his uniform on days off.

Near the town train station...

The front part of his Regent-style haircut.

EE EEE EE!!

YA KNOW, I BEEN PRETTY LUCKY UP TO NOW.

I HAD ALL I CAN TAKE!

CHIEF!!

THE ONLY WAY TO DELIVER A PASSIONATE LOVE LETTER...

...IS A MESSAGE ARROW!!

JUST LIKE THIS!

The sound. **WHAT HO?!**

MURDEROUS INTENT!!

MANGOKU, GO FORTH!

Harima watches the same show as Tenma.

UWAAAAAA?!!!

WOOO

VWRR

Harima Kenji: Slow Motion.

SST

AND ANOTHER...

WHAT'S GOING ONNN?!

BASH

VRRRR

FAREWELL

HORSEBACK-STYLE ARCHERY FROM A BUS ROOF.

VRR

UPPER YAGAMI-SAKA HILL

46

RR

RR

RR

I CAN'T LOSE HOPE!

WOBBLE

NOW'S MY CHANCE!!

MY TARGET'S STANDING STILL!

VWA

RR

FIN

ZANNG

WIN!

VEEEEN

TMP TMP

AH! KARASUMA-KUN'S GOING INTO A BANK!

OKAY, KARASUMA-KUN! PREPARE TO MEET YOUR DESTINY!!

IT'S WRONG! IT ALL WENT SO WRONG!!

→ Surprised.

AMAZING!!

ARCHERY HIGH SCHOOL COED!

Thieves Hold Up Bank With Model Gun

#13 .... Fin.

THE WORLD'S BIGGEST FOOL FOR TENMA!

Osakabe Itoko introduces...

HARI　MA　KEN　JI
播磨拳児

STATS:

Height: 180 cm (5' 11")

Favorite Thing: Curry

Least Favorite Thing: Shellfish, study

Favorite Actor: Yakushamaru Kôji (plays Mangoku)

Favorite Song: I'm always hearing the theme song from "Project A."

Special Talent: Fighting

Weak Point: Dim-witted

Notes: During his middle-school years, he was so much trouble nobody could do a thing with him, but nowadays he's a lot quieter.

One Last Word: He needs to pay his rent by the end of each month!

♯14 SPEED

WE'RE TOO OLD FOR FIELD TRIPS! USE "RECREATION," THAT'S THE PROPER WORD.

"FIELD TRIP"? REMINDS ME OF GRADE SCHOOL.

YAAAY! A FIELD TRIP!

SAME THING.

I'LL SAY!!

WHERE IS HE SUPPOSED TO BE GOING?

SHK SHK

AH! IT'S KARASUMA-KUN!

IT LOOKS LIKE HE'S GOT A SPECIAL ASSIGNMENT TODAY.

YOU'RE SAYING THAT WHEN THE BUS STOPS, WE ALL GOTTA CHANGE SEATS?

WHY DO SWEET SNACKS TASTE SO MUCH BETTER ON DAYS LIKE THIS?

Inside the bus ...

I DON'T NEED IT. I'LL PASS.

THE REASONING SEEMS TO BE THAT THE GIRLS SHOULD ENGAGE IN CONVERSATION WITH THE LESS FAMILIAR BOY CLASSMATES TO INCREASE OVER-ALL CLASS MORALE.

Tsukamoto Tenma: Snack Food Bill, ¥500.

RIGHT! I MUST BE IN THE SEAT NEXT TO KARASUMA-KUN!!

THIS IS NO TIME FOR EATING PICKY STICKS!

MNCH MNCH MNCH MNCH

TH-THAT'S IT!

AS YOU MUNCH YOUR SNACKS, YOU SEEM UNDER A LETHARGY... *I'LL REVIVE YOU!!*

MMM... TENMA-CHAN!

Harima's love at work.

I *WILL* SIT BESIDE HER TODAY!!

SHK

MUNCH MUNCH MUNCH

YOU'RE JUST LIKE A SQUIRREL. THE WAY YOU'RE EATING THOSE.

I-I'M A LITTLE NERVOUS.

GLANCE

RMMMM

As a wide variety of thoughts and intentions intermingle within the bus, the journey begins.

However...

HA HA HA HA

あはは

EH?!

オオーッ!!

RRRRN

・・・・・・・・・・・・

CHATTER

わい

I SURE AM!

ARE YOU SERIOUS?

CHATTER

KA-TUMP KA-TUMP

Harima Kenji: *Puts in the Homework.*

I CAUGHT THE WRONG BUS!!

HEY, YOUNGSTER! IF YOU CAUGHT THE EYE OF TSURU-SAN, THEN YOU MUST BE ONE IMPRESSIVE KIDDO!

MAKES ME WANT TO ADOPT YOU!

YEAH, THANKS.

Flower Playing Cards

WHAT A SPLENDID YOUNG MAN YOU ARE!

AND SUCH A CUTE CHILD.

NOOO!!

AND THIS OLD GUY'S PRETTY GOOD AT CARDS, TOO!

NOW'S MY CHANCE!

TMP

FINALLY! THE SEAT NEXT TO KARASUMA-KUN IS EMPTY!

GRRRMM

BAMP

WHY DON'T I SIT NEXT TO HIM?

OWWW!

Meanwhile, Tenma-chan is ...

HOW AWFUL!!

HI, KARASUMA-KUN.

CAN I SIT NEXT TO YOU?

FINE.

YOU'LL HAVE THE SHAKIEST SEAT ON THE BUS!

YOU'LL BE TOO SICK TO STAY!

ONE SHOULD BEWARE OF THE CURSE OF ONE IN LOVE!!

ONE DIGS TWO GRAVES WITH THIS CURSE STUFF!

BUT I MADE MYSELF EVEN SICKER THAN I DID HER!

I'M FEELING A LITTLE CARSICK.

I DID IT!

VICTORY!

SEE YOU LATER, KARASUMA-KUN.

HM?

I HAVE TO TAKE THAT ONE STEP TO GET CLOSER TO KARASUMA-KUN!

AT LEAST LET ME DIE IN HIS ARMS!

BUT THIS IS MY LAST CHANCE!!

EVEN IF I PASS OUT...

WOBBLE

WOBBLE

Sawachika Eri: Dirty Trick Victim.

B-BMP
B-BMP

U-UM...
KARASUMA-KUN?

UFF!

I'M FINALLY SITTING NEXT TO HIM! I WANT TO SAY SOMETHING, BUT MY HEART'S BEATING TOO FAST.

I-I'M THE BUS DRIVER. BUT DON'T WORRY ABOUT ME. I'M JUST A LITTLE CARSICK.

PANT

WHEEZE

M-MISTER, WHO THE HECK ARE YOU?!

HERE HE IS!

KARASUMA-KUN!! WHERE ARE YOU?!

HUH?! THEN WHERE DID KARASUMA-KUN GO OFF TO?!

GRMMM

14 .... Fin.

**Harima Kenji
introduces ...**

KARASU MA Ô JI
烏丸大路

STATS:

Height: Dunno. A little shorter than me. 175 cm (5' 9") maybe?

Favorite Thing: Dunno

Least Favorite Thing: Dunno

Special Talent: Probably being judgmental. Aside from that, I hear he's good at school.

Hair Style: Really weird, huh?

Name: I always thought it was Torimaru.

Distinguishing Feature: He's always sitting alone spacing out.

Notes: He'll be transferring away in a year. For me, that's perfect timing!

One Last Word: I got no idea what he's thinking, but I don't think he's all that annoying.

#15 RAIN MAN

At the exit...

SHHHHHH

MIKOTO... YOU'RE PRETTY TALL.

I'M NO SHORTY MYSELF.

YOU'RE ABOUT 172-173 CM (5' 8")?

NO, I'M NOT.

PEOPLE ALWAYS ASK.

I'M PRETTY CLOSE TO THAT, THOUGH.

OH, HELL!

FORGOT MY UM-BRELLA.

THE RAINY SEASON'S STARTING, HUH?

HP...
SHHHH

SORRY 'BOUT THAT.

WE CAN BOTH FIT UNDER MINE.

QUITE THE CONTRARY. I'M NEARLY CERTAIN TSUKAMOTO-SAN HAS AN UMBRELLA ON HAND.

THEREFORE, WE CAN LEAVE WITHOUT REGRET.

YOU THINK IT'S ALL RIGHT IF WE DON'T WAIT FOR TSUKAMOTO?

SHE SAID THAT SHE'S GOT ERRANDS, BUT...

NO DOUBT SHE FORGOT TO BRING HER UMBRELLA, TOO.

RIGHT! EVERY-BODY'S GONE HOME!

SHHHHH

KONNYAKU! I WANT TO EAT SOME KONNYAKU!

HOW DO YOU KNOW?

INTUITION.

I REALLY DIDN'T HAVE ERRANDS.

SORRY, EVERY-BODY.

SHHHH

IT'S REALLY COMING DOWN.

A MELAN-CHOLY RAIN.

I REALLY DO HAVE MY UMBRELLA! YAKUMO MADE SURE THAT I HAD ONE.

HEH HEH HEH! YOU UNDER-ESTIMATE ME, MIKOTO-CHAN!

SEE!

BUT I...

BUT...

THIS DAY... THIS RAINY DAY IS SOMETHING I'VE BEEN WAITING A LONG TIME FOR!

I HAD SOMETHING I COULDN'T PUT OFF!

THERE WILL BE NO MISTAKES TODAY!

SHAKIIN

...WE'LL SHARE THIS UMBRELLA!

KARASUMA-KUN AND I...

GONNG

ZLIPP

OH!

JUST YOU WAIT, KARASUMA-KUN!

FWOOM

AH!

FWOOM

ZZAKK

Lunging at full power.

THIS STUPID THING! THIS STUPID THING.

I FORGOT THE MOST IMPORTANT PART!!

THAKK

THAKK

THAT HURTS...

OHH, NOOO!!

IF KARA-SUMA BROUGHT HIS UM-BRELLA, THIS IS ALL USELESS!

EH?

I'M SO SORRY!!

DRIP DRIP

DLLOPP DLLOPP

NO, IT'S OKAY...

KYAAAAAH!! KARASUMA-KUN?!?!

DO YOU HAVE AN...

...UM-BRELLA?

B-BY THE WAY, KARASUMA-KUN! THERE'S SOMETHING I WANT TO ASK...

UM... UH...

FIDGET

FIDGET

IF YOU DON'T MIND, WE COULD SHARE...

I-I HAVE MY UMBRELLA WITH ME!

...RIGHTY!!

ALL...

I'M AFRAID NOT.

...COAT!

RAIN...

I BROUGHT...

...MY RAINCOAT AND GEAR.

YUP!
YUP!
YUP!

S-SURE! MODERN HIGH-SCHOOL STUDENTS BRING RAIN-COATS THESE DAYS!

THAT'S KARASUMA-KUN FOR YOU! TWO STEPS AHEAD OF THE NORMAL STUDENT!

BUT THAT'S WHY I LOVE HIM!

HUH? YOU BROUGHT AN UMBRELLA, TOO? WHO CARES! LET'S SHARE MY UMBRELLA ANYWAY!

HUH?!

B-BUT WHAT'LL I DO? THAT MEANS THAT KARASUMA-KUN AND I WILL NEVER SHARE AN UMBRELLA!

ONE PUSH TO GET YOUR WAY, HUH?

OH, SO THAT'S IT!

NOD NOD NOD

I GUESS I GOT NO CHOICE.

YOU MEAN USE ONLY ONE UMBRELLA ON PURPOSE?!

I'VE *ALWAYS* WANTED TO DO THAT! YOU'LL LIKE IT! I PROMISE! ♥

K-KARASUMA-KUN! I-I HAVE A FAVOR TO ASK YOU...

WHOOSH

C-COULD YOU PLEASE GO WITH ME UNDER MY UMBRELLA?

I P-PROMISE I'LL LIKE IT! I-I MEAN, YOU'LL LIKE IT!

Tsukamoto Tenma: *Hang in There*

...AND
GEAR... RAIN-
COAT...

I've completely forgotten the
countdown, but Karasuma-kun has only
302 days left before the transfer!!

#15.........Fin.

Tonight everybody's having a sleepover at Tenma's house...

#16 WILD PARTY

SO I'M GOING TO GET EVERYONE A LITTLE WASTED AND ASK THEM ALL SORTS OF THINGS!

I FINALLY GET MY PAJAMA PARTY!

どぅん THUD

IT'S JUST A LITTLE BIT. IT'LL BE OKAY.

ARE YOU *REALLY* GOING TO BREAK OUT THE BEER?

THESE ARE FUN EVERY ONCE IN A WHILE.

ガッ!! GRR RRN

AHHH! THAT WAS A GOOD BATH.

NONE FOR ME. I DON'T DRINK.

HERE, AKIRA-CHAN!

NO, IT'S ALWAYS BEEN WINE AND WHISKEY.

YOU'RE KIDDING!!

I'VE BEEN WAITING FOR THAT!

I BROUGHT SOME BEERS!

I'VE ALWAYS WANTED TO TRY BEER.

DON'T GET TOO CONFIDENT, MIKOTO-CHAN!

..."POPS"...?

SURE, POPS ALWAYS WANTS ME DRINKING WITH HIM NIGHTS.

THE OLD BAG'S ALWAYS HOLLERING AT HIM ABOUT IT, THOUGH! HA HA HA!

OH, COME ON! IS EVERYBODY WEIRD?

MIKOTO, ARE YOU A GIRL WHO CAN HOLD HER LIQUOR?

OKAY, THEN...

KAMPAI!!

WELL! YOU'RE QUITE THE DRINKER!

SEE? I HAVE A BOTTLE SET UP JUST FOR ME!

EHEM... B-BY THE WAY...

GLUG GLUG... GLUG GLUG

Funnel

I HAVE TO. SHE'S A WIMP WITH ALCOHOL.

Tenma's specially-made bottle contains mostly Oolong tea set up by Yakumo.

— 133 —

Tsukamoto Yakumo: Loves the Period Pieces.

Takano Akira: *Knows Just About Everything.*

I'VE HEARD OF A METHOD CALLED *THE HANGING BRIDGE EFFECT.*

HUH? WH-WHAT'S THAT? IT SOUNDS INTERESTING!

H-HOW ABOUT YOU, AKIRA-CHAN? ABOUT SAYING HOW YOU FEEL...

AWWW...

I DOUBT YOU'D WANT TO USE THIS METHOD, BUT...

EH?! O-OH, REALLY?

NEITHER HAVE I. AND I NEVER INTEND TO TRY EITHER.

I NEVER TRIED IT, SO I DON'T KNOW.

THE BRAIN MISTAKES FOR LOVE WHAT IS ACTUALLY NOTHING MORE THAN THE BEATING OF ONE'S HEART FROM FEAR.

Sees opposite sex.

Causes hallucination.

B-BMP

B-BMP

Afraid of the wobbly bridge.

"IF ONE WALKS ACROSS A HANGING BRIDGE AND SEES A MEMBER OF THE OPPOSITE SEX, ONE FALLS IN LOVE." OR SO THEY SAY.

IN SIMPLE TERMS, THAT'S ABOUT IT.

HMM... SO WHAT YOU'RE SAYING IS IF A GUY IS REALLY SCARED AT THE MOMENT HE LOOKS AT YOU, HE'LL FALL IN LOVE WITH YOU? DID I GET THAT RIGHT?

EH?! REALLY?! TELL ME! TELL ME HOW!!

IT'S SO EASY TO HAVE SOMEONE FALL IN LOVE WITH YOU.

AS A PSYCHOLOGICAL THEORY. DON'T COUNT ON IT IN REAL LIFE.

IS THAT REAL?

STBB STBB

HYUUUUU

RoofTop

KARASUMA-KUN... ...I LOVE YOU!!

LOOK, YOU'RE ABOUT TO FALL! YOU'RE GONNA FALL!

— 135 —

IT'S SOMETHING EVEN ANIMALS CAN DO!

DRESS YOURSELF UP! IT WORKS FOR THE PEACOCK, DOESN'T IT?

THERE'S SUCH A THING AS CLOTHES, ISN'T THERE?

ARE YOU STUPID OR SOMETHING?

THAT DISPLAY IS ALSO MEANT TO THREATEN OTHERS. BESIDES, THAT'S THE MALE.

THAT ONLY WORKS FOR PEOPLE LIKE YOU, ERI-CHAN.

CLUELESS

ALL YOU HAVE TO DO IS BE PRETTY!

YOU'VE GOT ONE OF YOUR WEIRD IMAGES IN YOUR HEAD, DON'T YOU?

ARE YOU SURE ABOUT THIS?

...I LOVE YOU!

WHOOSH

KARA-SUMA-KUN...

PEACOCK?

JUST BELIEVE IN YOURSELF, THEN GO OUT AND CRASH RIGHT INTO THE ONE YOU WANT!!

FOR HUMAN-KIND, IT'S ALL ABOUT HEART! WHAT'S INSIDE!

WHAT NOW, MIKOTO?

YOU DON'T GET IT AT ALL, PRINCESS!

THUNK

JUST CRASH INTO THE ONE I WANT, RIGHT?

GAMPH

THANK YOU! I'VE GOT COURAGE NOW!

Y-YOU'RE SO RIGHT, MIKOTO-CHAN!!

MOVED

Suō Mikoto: *Drinks Like a Fish.*

YOU'RE NOT GETTING MY MEANING AT ALL!

NO FAIR, MIKOTO-CHAN! YOUR CHEST IS BIG ENOUGH TO CRASH INTO SOMEONE!

. . . .

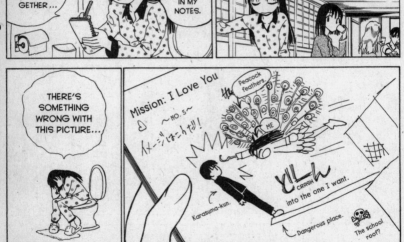

IF I TAKE EVERYTHING THEY JUST SAID AND PUT IT TO-GETHER...

BEFORE I FORGET, I'LL PUT THESE DOWN IN MY NOTES.

NOW MY COURAGE IS ALL MELTING AWAY... AND I'VE GOTTA GO TO THE BATHROOM.

THERE'S SOMETHING WRONG WITH THIS PICTURE...

Mission: I Love You

~NO. 5~

Peacock feathers.

ME

CRASH into the one I want.

Karasuma-kun.

Dangerous place.

The school roof?

WHO IN THE WORLD WOULD ACTUALLY GO THROUGH WITH SUCH A STUPID-LOOKING PLAN AS THAT?! I'M A DUMMY FOR EVEN THINKING IT!

OH... I QUIT!

That's who.

HYUUU

IT'S A MAN'S DUTY TO ACCEPT ANY CHALLENGE, AS LONG AS THERE IS EVEN A 1 % CHANCE OF SUCCESS!

MAYBE I'M WRONG. I'LL BET IT ISN'T JUST A MAN'S DUTY, BUT A HUMAN BEING'S DUTY!

IF I WAIT LONG ENOUGH, MAYBE THEY'LL HOLD A "BIRDMAN" CONTEST.

SAYING "I LOVE YOU" IS REALLY HARD.

16 . . . . Fin.

♭01　WONDER WOMAN

AH...

TSUKAMOTO YAKUMO
THE MAIN CHARACTER OF THIS STORY.
A VERY RESPONSIBLE YOUNGER SISTER
WHO WAS IN THE KITCHEN FROM 6:00
A.M. MAKING BREAKFAST AND FILLING
THE LUNCH BOXES FOR HER SISTER
AND HERSELF.

MMM...

GOOD
MORNING.

ᴙᴙᴙᴙN.
MORN-
ING.

TSUKAMOTO TENMA
YAKUMO'S BIG SISTER, STILL IN HER PAJAMAS.
IN THE REGULAR STORY, SHE'S THE MAIN
CHARACTER. SHE CAN BOAST OF IMPREGNABLE
DEFENSES THAT WILL PREVENT ANYONE FROM
WAKING HER UNTIL THE LAST MOMENT BEFORE
SHE IS DOOMED TO BE LATE FOR SCHOOL.

HM? I WONDER WHY...

HUH? THAT'S UNUSUAL.

YOUR BENTO LUNCH BOX IS IN THE KITCHEN. BREAKFAST IS ON THE TABLE.

I'M HEADING OUT A LITTLE EARLY TODAY.

THERE ARE *THREE* BENTO BOXES?

THERE'S YAKUMO... AND ME... WHO'S THE THIRD FOR?

? SEE YOU LATER.

TAKE CARE!

GO, YAKUMO, GO! ♥

THE BOY SHE LOVES?!

I'LL HAVE TO TAIL HER AND FIND OUT WHO HE IS FOR MYSELF!

NOW I'M WORRIED!

I HOPE NO BAD MAN IS TRYING TO TRICK HER.

BUT UNLIKE ME, SHE'S SO NAÏVE!

I'LL HAVE TO WATCH OVER HER WITH A WARM HEART.

SO NOW YAKUMO IS IN LOVE...

A BENTO LUNCH BOX FOR A CAT?!

BUG?

NO, A CAT.

I THOUGHT FOR SURE YOU HAD CAUGHT THE BUG!

NEE-CHAN...

YOU KNOW, YOU REALLY DIS-APPOINT ME!

SO... A STRAY CAT, HUH?

HAVE YOU BEEN LOOKING AFTER IT LONG?

YEAH, BUT...

AH!

VWIP

— 142 —

HONESTLY, YAKUMO! WHAT DO YOU DO THIS FOR?!

I'LL LEAVE YOUR BENTO FOR YOU HERE.

IT'S JUST BEING CAUTIOUS.

DUMB CAT, TRYING TO ACT COOL!

IT WASN'T NICE TO YOU AT ALL!

IT JUST IGNORED YOU AND WENT AWAY!

FORGET THE CAT! TRY OUT LOVE AT LEAST ONCE!

IT'S JUST SOMETHING I WANT TO TRY OUT.

AH! WE'RE GOING TO BE LATE! LET'S GET TO SCHOOL, YAKUMO!

STUDENT C
SHE'S REALLY GOT STYLE!

STUDENT D
IS SHE REALLY THE MOST POPULAR OF ALL THE NEW STUDENTS?

STUDENT A
ISN'T THAT TSUKAMOTO, THE FIRST-YEAR STUDENT?

STUDENT B
MAN, IS SHE CUTE!

STUDENT E

IT ISN'T JUST HER LOOKS. SHE'S GOT THE BODY OF A REAL ATHLETE!

DURING GYM CLASS THE TEACHER IN CHARGE OF TRACK AND FIELD SCOUTED HER OUT.

MAYBE, BUT IF SO...

7 Minami Shingo

8 Tsukamoto Yak

9 Yoshino Aya

SO THEY *DO* EXIST! THE "PERFECT WOMAN" THAT WE'RE ALWAYS HEARING ABOUT.

STUDENTS E & F

IT TURNS OUT SHE'S REALLY SMART, TOO. SHE PLACED 8TH IN THE MID-TERMS.

ALL THE BOYS ARE AFTER HER, HUH?

WHAT? IS SHE JUST TOO PICKY?

...SHE WON'T HAVE ANYTHING TO DO WITH THEM.

YOU'RE *SURE* YOU FELT SOME-ONE'S EYES ON YOU?

THEN I'D BE REALLY CAREFUL IF I WERE YOU.

?

THAT CAT. OR DID I JUST IMAGINE IT?

IT'S ALMOST LIKE SHE'S NOT AWARE OF ALL THE ATTENTION.

AW! WHATTA WASTE!

THE ONE UGLY POINT ABOUT TSUKAMOTO YAKUMO.

ARE YOU SAYING THAT THE CAT RETURNS TO PAY BACK A KINDNESS?

THOSE THINGS DON'T HAPPEN IN THE REAL WORLD!

OH, COME ON! THAT'S TOO MUCH LIKE A FAIRY-TALE!

NO, A CAT...

COME ON! YOU'LL BE LATE!

1-D

THEY DON'T... YOU'RE RIGHT. THEY DON'T, HUH?

...Tsukamoto Yakumo was a little different than usual.

That entire day...

HERE. I'LL GET IT FOR YOU.

AH!

!

"In what way," you ask?

PLUNK

THIS **MUST** BE MY *LUCKY DAY!*

OHHH! I WAS ABLE TO *TOUCH* TSUKAMOTO!

If anyone likes Yakumo, she can hear the whisper of his heart.

But to a girl as hopeless at love as Yakumo is, it doesn't help at all.

THANK YOU. : : :

She understands the sentiment, but she has no idea how to respond.

MAYBE I ACTUALLY MADE A GOOD IMPRESSION!

Y E S!

SHE LOOKS SO GROWN UP, TOO!

GOOD LIE! EH HEH HEH!

NOW... I'M GONNA TAKE HER ALL THE WAY!

I'VE NOTICED WHAT A HARD WORKER YOU ARE!

I WAS HOPING YOU'D JOIN US ON THE STUDENT COUNCIL!

EH? I, UM...

TSUKAMOTO-SAN, RIGHT?

After school...

UH... YEAH, I...

WE'LL BE ALONE IN THE STUDENT COUNCIL ROOM,

BATHED IN THE LIGHT OF THE SETTING SUN!

IT'S FOR THE SAKE OF THE SCHOOL!

I JUST KNOW YOU WANT TO MAKE A DIFFERENCE, DON'T YOU?!

STOP THAT RIGHT NOW! YOU'RE SCARING THE POOR GIRL!

OWWW!!

THE FIRST STEP IS TO COME TO THE STUDENT COUNCIL ROOM AND HAVE A QUICK LOOK AROUND. LET'S GO!

BUT... I'M EXPECTED HOME RIGHT AFTER SCHOOL...

I'LL GET RIGHT TO THE POINT!

MY NAME IS HANAI HARUKI.

I'M THE AIKIDO CLUB PRESIDENT!

TSUKAMOTO-KUN, WOULD YOU LIKE TO LEARN *AIKIDO*?

AND I'M IN THE SAME GRADE AS YOUR SISTER, TSUKAMOTO TENMA.

SHUMP

OH, IT'S HANAI-KUN, AGAIN?

SHFF SHFF

I THINK IT **REALLY** WOULD **SUIT YOU!**

I THINK A MARTIAL ARTS HAKAMA WOULD SUIT YOU FINE!

I—

I...

This is a man whose words and thoughts match nearly perfectly. Yakumo has never met such a man before.

But that doesn't mean that she's in *love* or anything!

ガァン!

VWAM

I'M SORRY, BUT MARTIAL ARTS AREN'T FOR ME...

I'LL GRAB HER RIGHT ARM.

FOR EXAMPLE, IF I...

SST

THE PROTECTIVE ARTS ARE VERY EFFECTIVE AGAINST LEWD ATTACKERS!

I'LL GRAB HER LEFT ARM.

WHOOSH

OKAY, THEN...

?
YOU WERE ABLE TO AVOID ME?

SWIPP

スカッ

スカッ

SWIPP

SHASH

SWIPP

WHAT'S GOING ON?! I CAN'T TOUCH HER AT ALL!

SWIPP

It's easy for her to avoid him, since she can read his mind.

HOW CAN YOU BE SO FAST WHEN YOUR SISTER IS SUCH A FRIGGIN' DOLT!?

AH!

ZWAAA

WHAMM

!

When she hears her sister being bad-mouthed, Yakumo finally gets serious.

I— I'M SORRY...

AH!

YAKUMO! THE FLAME!

YOU'LL SPOIL THE SAUCE!

I HOPE IT'S ALL RIGHT.

UH...

• • • • •

CHEER UP YAKUMO!

BUT IT'S TIME TO

I DON'T UNDERSTAND ANY OF THIS,

YOU DON'T MIND, DO YOU?

EH?

YAKUMO, LET'S HAVE SOMETHING UNUSUAL ON THE MENU TODAY!

It looks like Yakumo can hear the whispers of Tenma's heart, too.

NEE-CHAN...

AND IN MY RIGHT WILL BE BANANA DAIFUKU CAKES!

I'LL PUT KETCHUP IN MY LEFT HAND

• • • • •

LEFT.

WHICH ONE?

I'LL PUT TWO OF MY FAVORITE INGREDIENTS ON THESE CARDS, AND YOU CHOOSE ONE AT RANDOM.

OKAY. WHAT DO YOU WANT TO HAVE?

To Yakumo, her sister has no faults.

NEE-CHAN... YOU MADE A MISTAKE. ABOUT WHICH HAND HELD WHAT CARD.

← A HUGE SWEETS-AHOLIC.

Banana Daifuku Cakes.

♪ NO I DIDN'T!

Banana Daifuku Cakes.

...the one who loves her big sister the best. At least right now.

NOW THAT'S AN ODD SMELL...

AH!

GUCH GUCH

In the end, Tsukamoto Yakumo is...

OH! IT'S UNUSUAL FOR YOU TO WORRY ABOUT WHAT YOU PUT INTO YOUR COOKING.

I HAVE NO CHOICE. I'LL HAVE TO ADD THEM...

...TO THE CURRY.

Tenma does chores.

PLOOMP PLOOMP

YOU THINK SO? I THINK IT ISN'T HALF BAD.

THEN...

TASTES AWFUL...

ARE YOU HERE?

HERE'S DINNER.

YOU CAN'T GET DOWN, RIGHT?

COME TO ME!

SHUUSH

MYAAOW!

MYAAOW!

UP IN THE TREE?

ZLIPP

SLOWLY... TAKE YOUR TIME...

THAT'S IT...

WHOOSH

ARE YOU ALL RIGHT?

OWW... ・・・・・・

AH!

I HEARD!

MYAOW!

MEOWW.

LICK LICK

YOU KNOW, I CAN READ PEOPLE'S THOUGHTS SOMETIMES.

I WAS WONDERING WHAT YOU'D SAY IN YOUR HEART, SO I WAS HOPING I'D HEAR YOU TOO.

BUT I GUESS IN A CAT'S HEART, YOU GUYS JUST SAY MEOW, MEOW, HUH?

TOO BAD.

♭ 01 .... Fin.

A MONTH AGO ON THE WAY TO THE BIG GUY'S PLACE, I SAW THIS GIRL...

SHE WAS REALLY PRETTY AND HAD THIS WEIRD LOOK IN HER EYES.

♭02 RAINY DAYS AND MONDAYS

WE HAVE TO GO COMPLAIN TO THE THUN-DER GOD.

CAN'T HAVE THE RAIN CONTINUE LIKE THIS.

WE CAN'T PUT OUR LAUNDRY OUT ON THE LINE LIKE THIS.

SHHHH

NO LUCK. IT ISN'T GOING TO STOP.

WELL?

HM? WHAT IS IT, YAKUMO?

I SEE A THUNDER KID.

TREMBLE TREMBLE

ハァ... SHHH

HUH?

AT OUR GATE...

WHAT ARE YOU DOING HERE?

THE RAIN GOT YOU PRETTY GOOD, HUH?

SST

TWITCH

YOU'LL...

... CATCH COLD.

UH...

EH?! AH! NO!

I'M NOT DOING ANYTHING WRONG! I JUST GOT HERE BY ACCIDENT!

THE GAME OF GO.

I DON'T KNOW HOW TO PLAY!!

THAT TAUGHT YOU YOUR PLACE, RIGHT?

FLIP FLIP
はた はた

SST

!

パフ?...

FFT?...

B-BMP

B-BMP

B-BMP

ちら...
GLANCE

N-NOTHING'S WRONG.

B-BMP

B-BMP

B-BMP

‥‥

WHAT'S WRONG?

B-BMP

|
!?

YAKUMO-
NEE-CHAN

REALLY IS

BEAUTIFUL!

I JUST
NEVER KNOW
WHAT TO DO.

I THOUGHT-IF
I CAME HERE,
*I MIGHT
SEE HER.*

BUT
IT ISN'T LIKE
I PLANNED
ANYTHING.

*YAKUMO-
NEE-CHAN
IS JUST SO*

BEAUTIFUL!

...YAKUMO...
NEE-CHAN...

I...
I REALLY DIDN'T
RUN AWAY FROM
HOME. SORRY
I LIED.

!

SHFF

*I ALWAYS
NOTICE HER.*

I WANT TO
BE WITH HER
ALL THE
TIME!

I JUST
WANTED TO BE
WITH HER.

*SO
WARM!*

WHEN SHE DOESN'T, I WISH SHE'D **TURN AROUND** AND **LOOK AT ME.** I JUST FEEL **SO HELPLESS.**

UM...

ちらっ
GLANCE

YOU CALL **THAT** TAKING CARE OF A GUY?

DON'T FORGET OUR KICKBACK FOR FEEDING YOU AND PUTTING YOU UP FOR THE NIGHT.

SHŪJI-KUN?

N-NO, IT'S NOTHING! OKAY, SEE YA.

I WANT TO COME BACK,

BUT I CAN'T SAY IT!

...BUT HE SURE LIVENED UP A BORING EVENING, HUH, YAKUMO?

THE KID'S GOT THE WORST ATTITUDE...

...ANYTIME YOU FEEL LIKE IT.

COME BACK...

HUH?

HEY, BIG GUY! ARE YOU IN HERE! I FINALLY DECIDED TO DROP BY.

OH, SHŪJI! HOW'S IT HANGING, COUSIN?

YEAH.

♭02 .... Fin.

To be continued in Volume 2

About the Creator

Jin Kobayashi was born in Tokyo. *School Rumble* is his first manga series. He has answered these questions from his fans.

What is your hobby?
Basketball

Which manga inspired you to become a creator?
Dragon Ball

Which character in your manga do you like best?
Kenji Harima

What type of manga do you want to create in the future?
Action

Name one book, piece of music, or movie you like.
The Indiana Jones series

Translation Notes

Japanese is a tricky language for most Westerners, and translation is often more art than science. For your edification and reading pleasure, here are notes on some of the places where we could have gone in a different direction in our translation of the work, or where a Japanese cultural reference is used.

Family or Personal Names
Most students in a Japanese classroom are identified by their family names, for example, Karasuma-kun. Even a close friend may use the last name, such as when Mikoto addresses Tenma, but you'll find that most people in a friendly relationship will use personal names.

Page 5, Second-Year High School Student
Japanese high schools are arranged a little differently than most American high schools. Grade school is grades 1–6; middle school is grades 7–9; and high school is grades 10–12. Since Tenma is in her second year of high school, she is the same age as juniors in American high schools.

Page 5, New School Year
Unlike American schools, which typically start the academic year in August or September, the Japanese school year begins in early April.

Page 6, How to Pronounce *Tsukamoto*

Many language teachers will tell you that in Japanese every syllable is pronounced. That is not entirely true; some vowel sounds nearly vanish. In the *tsu* sound of *Tsukamoto*, the *u* sound is hardly heard, so to sound more accurate, one should pronounce the name as if there were no *u* sound: Tskamoto.

Page 6, *Ôji*

Just a little Jin Kobayashi pun. Using different kanji, the pronunciation of Karasuma-kun's personal name, *Ôji*, also means prince.

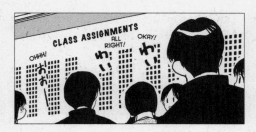

Page 6, New Class Assignments

Every new class year, homeroom assignments are posted on the school bulletin board, as is the case in American schools, but in Japan the stakes are higher. In Japanese schools, the students typically stay in the same room and the teachers move from class to class, so the students who are in your homeroom are the students you will see all day, every day, for nearly every class for the rest of the year.

Pages 11 and 12, Can't Write

In Japan, admitting that you love a person (*kokuhaku*) is almost a formalized ritual. One can leave a love letter in the shoe locker (see note), or just come out and say it. In Japanese one of the ways of saying it is, *"Watashi wa, anata ga suki desu."* Or simply, *"Suki desu."* The

usual word for love/like/having a crush is *suki*. There are other words, of course, but this is the one Tenma cannot seem to say. The Japanese words that came out of her pen were: *sukii*, to go skiiing; *sukippu*, skipping; *sukiyaki*, a kind of food; *suki ga nai*, to have good defenses; *sukiru-appu*, to improve your skills; and *sukinshippu*, skinship, or building a parental relationship with an infant through touch. The translation tried to take the first two letters of the word *love* and match the Japanese meanings as closely as possible. Still, as in the original, the words get further and further away from the one Tenma wants to write.

Page 13, Love Letters in the Shoe Locker

Leaving a love letter in a student's shoe locker is a longtime tradition in stories about school-age love (and probably has plenty of precedent in reality, but most likely not to the extent you find in romances). The shoe locker is one of the places where a student in love can be sure that the object of his or her affection will go at the start and end of each school day, so it is a favorite place to leave notes and especially love letters.

Page 20, Harry McKenzie

The Japanese pronunciation of the name Harry McKenzie sounds almost exactly the same as the name Harima Kenji.

Page 34, Sonko

The second kanji in Sun Tsu's name is also pronounced *ko* by the Japanese, and that same character can be found in many popular girls names such as Junko, Kyoko, Keiko, Yûko, Tomoko, etc. In fact, in post-war Japan it was the fashion to name female children with a name ending in *ko*. (This fashion has changed in the past ten to twenty years.) So when Tenma looks at the kanji for the name Sun Tsu (usually pronounced *Sonshi*, in Japan), she automatically thinks the book was written by Sonko, a woman.

THAT MAKES SENSE! ONLY A WOMAN WOULD KNOW THE SOUL OF ANOTHER GIRL!

SON KO?

孫子 ？
そん こ

SO WHO WROTE THIS TREATISE?

Page 36, Take Off Like a Hare

In Japanese this appeared as the kanji compound (two or more kanji put together to form a single word) *datto*, made up of the kanji for *undress* and *rabbit*. Since *datto* is not a very commonly used word in Japan, it wouldn't be unusual for a junior in high school to be unfamiliar with it.

Note: Sun Tsu does talk about running away like a rabbit, under certain circumstances.

Page 37, Beloved

The kanji that Tenma wanted Karasuma-kun to read for her was one that is pronounced *suki*, a homophone for the Japanese word for love, but this kanji means an opening in one's defenses. She wants to hear him say "I love you" to her, even if it's a trick. Since there are no good homophones for love that can be found in Sun Tsu's *Art of War*, I chose to make it a pronunciation of *beloved*, which is found in a section of *The Art of War* that advised generals to treat their soldiers like their own beloved children in order to foster loyalty.

Fortunately, *beloved* also sounds like an endearment an old-school boyfriend might use.

Page 38, Honey Extractor

There's another word pronounced the same as *love* in Japanese (*suki*) that means plow. So in the same vein, my mission was to find a word that would be an endearment (*honey*) but that would also have something to do with a tool that might be found on a farm.

Page 43, Learn from Others' Mistakes

The old Japanese proverb that Kenji used is one that translates to, "Instead of accusing others of bad behavior, learn from it and behave well yourself."

Page 45, Shampoos in the Morning

Most baths in Japanese households are taken at night. But there is a group of people who wash their hair in the morning, and these are given the name of *asashanha*.

Page 52, Wrote the Kanji Wrong

The left side of the final kanji character is incorrect. Tennôji wrote it with a radical indicating *man* rather than with the proper radical, which means left side.

Page 62, Mama-chari

These are what used to be called women's bicycles in the U.S. One-speed, or three-speed at best, a distinctive basket, and a traditional low-bar frame make up the standard bike ridden by housewives all over Japan. The name, *mama-chari*, comes from *mama* (mother) and the onomatopoeic sound of a bicycle bell, *charin charin*.

Page 63, Yagami-saka/Shisshin-saka

The kanji for arrow, *ya*, differs from the kanji for loss, *shitsu*, only by the elevation of the top horizontal line, so they are easily mistaken for each other. The author is giving the audience a clue that half-British Eri is still having a few problems with her kanji.

Page 76, Measurements Check

A measurements check or physical checkup (*shintai-sokutei*) is conducted at the beginning of the school year to record the physical condition of each student. Height, weight, sitting height, and chest circumference are some of things that may be checked. These checks are started in the first grade and

data is kept until the twelfth grade. Many schools also have monthly checkups for height and weight only, administered by the teachers.

IF THEY'RE SO WORKED UP TO SEE THAT KIND OF THING, THEY SHOULD JUST BECOME DOCTORS OR NURSEMAIDS.

Page 78, Nursemaids

The Japanese word that Eri said was *kangofu*, the most common Japanese word for nurse. But since the *fu* part means woman or wife, and there is an ever-increasing number of male nurses, a more politically correct word has come along, *kangoshi*, which does not specify gender.

Page 82, What in the World Is Gunpura?

Here's the answer to Mikoto's question. The *pura* part is a shortening of *purasuchikku*, which means plastic and refers to plastic models. *Gun* is short for Gundam (from the famous giant-robot TV franchise, "Mobile Suit Gundam"). So Akira's hobby is putting together the complex, high-quality, snap-together Gundam plastic model kits that are so popular in Japan.

Page 90, Ukiyo-e

Floating World drawings are generally found in intricate wood-block prints that were created starting late in the Edo Period (1603–1867) of Japan. They include stylized, impressionistic pictures based on Kabuki plays and the pleasure districts of Japan's largest cities such as Edo (Tokyo) and Kyoto.

Ukiyo-e.

Page 93, Buns

One of the quick snacks in Japan is prepackaged buns that the Japanese call by the same word they use for bread, *pan*. They are usually purchased in bakeries and grocery stores, but prepackaged *pan* can also be found in vending machines and other convenient locations. Most contain fillings such as curry, barbecued pork, sweet bean paste, and other varieties. Like chips or candy bars from vending machines in America, *pan* is an inexpensive snack that quite often substitutes for a meal.

Page 100, Uchidate Makiko

Uchidate Makiko is a prolific female writer of books and movies most famous for her TV dramas—eleven-episode stories, usually romantic, featuring plots that have twists and turns and, as with most television, aren't too challenging to the average viewer. (There are exceptional dramas out there, of course.)

Page 103, Hurricane Kick

In this case, Hurricane is spelled Hariken, and it's made up of two kanji, one being the first character in Harima's name and the second meaning fist.

GET 'EM, MANGOKU!!

Page 109 Three to Get Killed!

Sanbiki ga Kiru! (Three for the Kill!) is an immensely popular *jidai-geki* (Warring States or Edo Period drama) that starred the handsome Yakusho Kôji as the swordsman Sengoku. Sengoku's two companions are Tono-sama and Tako (*tono* means lord, and *tako* can mean octopus). In *School Rumble*, Tenma's favorite *jidai-geki*, *Sanbiki ga Kirareru!* (Three to Get Killed!), stars the handsome Yakushamaru Kôji (*yakusha* means actor) as the swordsman Mangoku (*sen* means 1,000, and *man* means 10,000). Mangoku's two companions are Ue-sama and Ika (*ue* means above, and *ika* can mean both below and eel).

Page 111, Boss Coffee

With its stylish jet-black can emblazoned with the image of an authoritative-looking man smoking a pipe and the name Boss in big, bold letters, there's no doubt that Suntory's Boss canned coffee is aimed at a male demographic.

BOSS COFFEE IS THE ONLY ONE FOR A MAN!

WHY DO SWEET SNACKS TASTE SO MUCH BETTER ON DAYS LIKE THIS?

Page 117, Picky Sticks

The Picky Sticks in Tenma's world are the Picky Sticks in ours. A favorite snack in Japan, and the almost-official Japanese snack food of otaku everywhere. They are thin, crunchy sticks of sweet bread covered in chocolate or other flavors.

Page 118, Old Maid

The game Karasuma and Harima are playing, *Babanuki* (which literally translates to Pulling Out Grandma), is basically Old Maid. Players take turns selecting a card from their opponent's hand, trying to make pairs and hoping not to choose the single joker in the deck. The loser is the person who winds up with the joker at the end of the game.

Page 123, Torimaru

The kanji for *Karasu* (raven or crow) differs from the kanji for *tori* (bird) by only one line. And the kanji for *ma* in Karasuma-kun's name is usually read *maru*. So thinking Karasuma-kun's name is Torimaru would be an easy mistake to make, especially for someone who doesn't pay much attention in kanji class.

Page 124, The Rainy Season and Romance

In Japan, it rains nearly every day in the month of June. This rainy season is called *tsuyu*, and it is a good idea to keep an umbrella handy. However, a couple walking home under a single umbrella is

the symbol for love in Japan. Like having two names in a heart in North America, two names under a stylized triangle (supposed to represent an

umbrella) means that the two people named are in love. The reason for this is because the Japanese are traditionally shy of physical intimacy in public, and two people can share a more intimate closeness under an umbrella than would normally be allowed.

Page 125, Konnyaku

Konnyaku is a traditional Japanese jelly-like health food made from a kind of potato called Konnyaku potato, containing calcium hydroxide extracted from eggshells.

Page 130, Rain Gear

The Japanese word for rain gear is *kappa*. But *kappa* is also a water sprite. Since there are no words for water sprite that also mean rain gear in English, this translation lets Karasuma-kun's oddness speak for itself.

Page 133, Kampai!

Alternatively spelled *Kanpai*, this toast literally means empty glass, but for all intents and purposes, its direct translation would be the English "Cheers!"

Page 142, Bug

Another pun. Tenma says, "I thought it was love," but she uses *koi*, another Japanese word for love. As anyone who owns a fish pond knows, *koi* can also mean those huge goldfish-like carp. So Yakumo's reply is, "Koi? No, it's a cat."

I THOUGHT FOR SURE YOU HAD CAUGHT THE BUG!

Page 145, The Cat Returns

Both the Studio Ghibli film and original manga by Hiiragi Aoi, *The Cat Returns*, are based on an old Japanese fairy tale titled *Neko no Ongaeshi* (The Cat Returns the Favor), about a cat who magically pays back a human for saving its life.

Page 151, Banana Daifuku Cakes

Banana daifuku is a *mochi* (rice paste) cake filled with sweet bean paste and a small chunk of banana.

Page 158, Shogi

Often called Japanese chess, shogi is a game with twenty pieces per player set on a nine-by-nine board. The object of the game is, as in chess, to capture the opponent's king.

Page 160, Yakumo-nee-chan

It is common for small children to call young (or young-looking) strangers "big brother" or "big sister." Shûji is using this form of address for Yakumo because he'd like a closer relationship with her, but it also reinforces in him that she is older and pretty much out of his league.

Preview of Volume 2

We're pleased to present you with a preview of *School Rumble*, Volume 2. This volume will be available in English on May 30, 2006, but for now you'll have to make do with Japanese!

黄色

辛かったろう！
だがそれも終わる！
よく聞くんだ！

発見！

播磨君
‥‥‥！？

天満ちゃーーん！！！

好…

な…

あぶ

ドドド

で

播磨拳児
全治十日

その日の記憶
不鮮明

なんだ
つけな
＜＜＜

ナンかすげー
良いことが
あった気が……

しかし君ほど
運の悪い男も
珍しいな…

サングラス
とり忘

播磨君
お見舞いに
来たよー

OH!?
ナゼ!?
ラッキー!!

■今鳥恭介■

痛かったっス

BY AKIRA SEGAMI

MISSION IMPOSSIBLE

The young ninja Kagetora has been given a great honor—to serve a renowned family of skilled martial artists. But on arrival, he's handed a challenging assignment: teach the heir to the dynasty, the charming but clumsy Yuki, the deft moves of self-defense and combat.

Yuki's inability to master the martial arts is not what makes this job so difficult for Kagetora. No, it is Yuki herself. Someday she will lead her family dojo, and for a ninja like Kagetora to fall in love with his master is a betrayal of his duty, the ultimate dishonor, and strictly forbidden. Can Kagetora help Yuki overcome her ungainly nature . . . or will he be overcome by his growing feelings?

Ages: 13 +

Special extras in each volume! Read them all!

VISIT WWW.DELREYMANGA.COM TO:
- Read sample pages
- View release date calendars for upcoming volumes
- Sign up for Del Rey's free manga e-newsletter
- Find out the latest about new Del Rey Manga series

GHOST HUNT

MANGA BY SHIHO INADA
STORY BY FUYUMI ONO

The decrepit building was condemned long ago, but every time the owners try to tear it down, "accidents" start to happen—people get hurt, sometimes even killed. Mai Taniyama and her classmates have heard the rumors that the creepy old high school is haunted. So, one rainy day they gather to tell ghost stories, hoping to attract one of the suspected spirits. No ghosts materialize, but they do meet Kazuya Shibuya, the handsome young owner of Shibuya Psychic Research, hired to investigate paranormal activity at the school. Also brought to the scene are an exorcist, a Buddhist monk, a woman who can speak with the dead, and an outspoken Shinto priestess. Surely one of them will have the talents to solve this mystery. . . .

Ages: 13 +

Special extras in each volume! Read them all!

VISIT WWW.DELREYMANGA.COM TO:
- Read sample pages
- View release date calendars for upcoming volumes
- Sign up for Del Rey's free manga e-newsletter
- Find out the latest about new Del Rey Manga series

TOMARE!

止まれ

[STOP!]

You're going the wrong way!

Manga is a completely different
type of reading experience.

To start at the *beginning*,
go to the *end*!

That's right! Authentic manga is read the traditional Japanese way—
from right to left. Exactly the *opposite* of how American books are
read. It's easy to follow: Just go to the other end of the book, and read
each page—and each panel—from right side to left side, starting at
the top right. Now you're experiencing manga as it was meant to be!

cy